Imagine Happiness

a simple guide

BOBBY SCHULLER

Dedicated to the *Happiness Hour* on the
Dennis Prager Show

Contents

CHAPTER ONE

The Fruit of Virtue

"Happiness is the settling of the soul into its
most appropriate spot."
—Aristotle

Lack of Happiness in a Happy-Driven Culture

I wanted to take my Grandpa Pursley to Spain.
That's how I ended up lying on a bed in a dark room in
Toledo, Spain—crying.

It's amazing how a man can find himself in a place
he thought would be mind-blowing, with people he
thought would make him happy, doing everything he
thought would be exciting, and yet finds himself caught
in an abyss of quiet desperation. The talking heads who

told him x, y, and z would make him happy were wrong. There's not enough money, travel, women, busy projects, exciting shows, or amazing experiences on earth to make him happy. It's impossible. That's what I realized one day when I was weeping alone in a cold, dark room in Spain.

Somehow I knew it was my duty to take my Grandpa Pursley to Spain. It was something he had earned, something he deserved but hadn't received. One day my Grandpa Pursley, who taught me what little Spanish I know, was sitting in my mom's living room and slammed his fist onto the old rocking chair saying, "I never went to Spain!" This was a startling moment for our little family who looked at my grandfather with genuine surprise. Typically a quiet man, he revealed a personal deep desire, an almost rite of passage never realized. My grandpa had traveled the world in the past, visiting many countries back when he ran a travel agency. Now he was chasing a new calling in his little classroom in south-central Los Angeles, teaching AP Spanish Literature to Central American students. With passion, he showed these kids the beauty of Spanish poetry and narrative. He would read to them about the shining knights of Toledo, but he had never been to the land of Don Quixote except in his imagination. Now, as he grew older, it was becoming a sour regret. After quiet reflection, I made him a solemn promise: I would get him, somehow, to Spain. So, I worked and saved, and, to everyone's surprise, we were on a plane only a few months later. My stepdad, Ron, came along and paid his own way, mostly to help my mom feel better about her eighty-two-year-old father wandering around Spain with her reckless son.

So my grandpa, my stepdad, and I were off on a little adventure to that beautiful country on the Castilian Peninsula. Truly, it was remarkable. We saw the works of Gaudí, bullfights, and ate tapas. We moved at an impressive pace by train and car, and we even hitchhiked once. We saw everything and anything of importance. It was going so well…until I found myself alone. Somehow there was a mix-up. My travel companions had set their return flight three days earlier than I had, and so I was doomed to spend three days by myself. That's how it started.

At first it was really nice. I was in Toledo, Spain. My eyes couldn't get enough of the medieval town that sat above the Tagus River. I was taken back to the sixth century as I strolled down a path of chaotic stones. The wind carried the scent of Toledo's famous Mazapán, causing me to salivate. I stopped to gaze at the town's centerpiece; the cathedral filled the sky around me. The baroque stones housed the art of Raphael and El Greco. That was the first day. On the second day, I found myself lying on a bed in a curtain-drawn room, weeping.

What on earth is happening to me? I thought, lying there staring at an old tube TV. It was tuned in to some infomercial but on mute. I was more than homesick, though it was that in part. I had gone from having the time of my life with my grandpa and Ron to being incredibly lonely. Surrounded by music, culture, and good food, I was in a place where I was supposed to be happy. I was in a castle. The weather was perfect. I could have done anything I wanted. I had complete freedom, but I was forlorn. My happiness had crashed into a chasm of loneliness. I had everything people told me I needed to be happy, but I wasn't.

I remembered a story from Henri Nouwen. Though I never met Henri in person, I've read his books and have listened to and even preached his sermons. He was like a mentor I never met, his words abiding deep within my heart. He wrote with vulnerability, even pain, about our loneliness and despair, about how God, our Father, loves and treasures us, and that somehow this love is all we need. Henri had an incredible career as a professor both at Harvard and Yale, with a number of bestselling books to his credit. And yet he ended his journey working with extremely handicapped people at L'Arche community in Canada as a way of practicing what it means to love others the way God loves us. He shouted his last words in his hospital bed, with hands lifted to the sky: "God is faithful! God is faithful!" It was his story I remembered in Toledo.

He was on a subway, and all around him were somber and lonely-looking people. Next to them were posters of beautiful people smiling and having fun.

They were selling happiness. The posters said, "eat me, visit me, sleep with me," but all around them were people who had been disappointed by the promise that eating something, visiting somewhere, or purchasing something, could make them happy.[i] They were being shuffled around the underground of a city where they were not valued and could be easily forgotten. They didn't understand that happiness can't come from anything external but materializes from something deeper. This "something deeper" is what got me out of bed the third and final day of my trip. It's what moved me from loneliness to happy solitude. The last day in Toledo was a pleasure, and I came home happy, not because of a trip, or food, or anything external, but because I had discovered something rich about life.

This is the age we live in. We are told happiness is for sale and all we need is the money to buy it. Like the poor souls on Henri's subway, we have spent the money, made the trip, and purchased the car or beautiful dress. We have filled our lives with events, stuff, noise, and pictures. Our lives are bursting with bright lights, but they're not illuminated. We're filled but unfulfilled, busy but unproductive. We have means, but no meaning. And still, like a boy scratching a mosquito bite, hoping the itch will go away, we consume, we find distractions, and we press on with unbridled restlessness. This is not the path to happiness.

Real happiness comes from a deeper place, not from anything external. The freshest and best water flows from the deepest, darkest chasms of the mountain. Likewise, true happiness flows from the hidden places of the human heart.

It is there God can build in us what Jesus calls "a wellspring of living water." However, it is not easy, it's not quick, and, like any wellspring, it requires a good bit of digging.

Happiness Is Not Pleasure

We human beings are experts at fooling ourselves. We play a silly game we all know is a farce, and yet we desperately hang onto it because it's all we really have. We behave as though fun, entertainment, a good love life, physical attractiveness, travel, and good food is what will make us happy. Getting the ability, the money, or the freedom to do these things and do them more often consumes our thoughts and our time. We are quietly angry with the people in our lives that hinder us from the pursuit of these pleasures. Sometimes we fantasize about simply flying away. The hope of someday "having it all" is almost a pleasure in itself. Of course, we have fond memories of enjoying these pleasures and indelibly link them to happiness. Eventually, happiness and pleasure are inseparable in our minds, and there we're trapped.

What we fail to realize is that pleasure did not make us happy. Rather, pleasure increased whatever happiness we already had. You were already happy when you got on that Jet Ski, but you were happier when you started going! You were happy when you left the house to go to dinner, but you were happier when you started eating. But if you had been unhappy when you sat down on that Jet Ski, or unhappy when you sat down for dinner, going out on the water or eating an amazing dinner didn't make you happy. In the times we enjoyed doing these things, we were probably already happy. Simply, these experiences increased the happiness we already had, but they didn't create it. It's so easy to forget the times we had the most interesting, best tasting, and most attractive things available to us…but were plagued with a nagging sense of unhappiness or boredom! And, like my experience in Spain, these things probably made us feel worse, because they were deconstructing the myth that pleasure and happiness are the same. Pleasure and happiness are not at all the same. Rather, pleasure is the sugar that swirls around in the fruit of happiness. Pleasure is the salt on the happiness French fries. Pleasure is the frame around the masterpiece we call happiness. In other words, happiness is pleasurable, and pleasure can increase our happiness in life, but pleasure cannot create happiness. They are not one in the same. We need only look to the real lives of our friends in Hollywood to know happiness and pleasure can exist miles apart from each other.

Pleasure is an important part of understanding a happy and meaningful life. I will write more about this in coming chapters, but for now, understand this: happiness and pleasure are not the same thing. That's why there are some happy people in prison, hospital beds, and homeless shelters, while there are some unhappy people in Las Vegas and Disneyland.

Happiness Is Not a Light Switch

It's possible that at one time or another, you have taken a long look in the mirror and asked, "Am I a happy person?" You have decided some people are happy and other people are not and have wondered which category you fit into. But is this the best way to think of happiness, as a light switch that is either on or off? The most recent research in the study of happiness suggests not. It's now believed that happiness is a dimmer switch rather than a light switch.

Most of us see happiness as something we either have or don't have, not as something we have more or less of. In other words, we wonder how to turn that switch on rather than how to turn the dimmer up. So, people wonder, "What will make me happy?" This is a mistake, because no one is completely happy or completely unhappy. Rather, people are happier and less happy. There is no limit to how happy a person can be, and there is no limit to how unhappy a person can be. This is exciting because, even if you are a very happy person, you can still, over time, become an even happier person! The goal, then, is not to discuss how we might be happy but instead how we can be happier than we are presently. The Harvard lecturer Tal Ben-Shahar says:

> "Am I happy?" is a closed question that suggests a binary approach to the pursuit of the good life: we are either happy or we are not. Happiness, according to this approach, is an end of a process, a finite definable point that, when reached, signifies the termination of the pursuit. This point, however, does not exist, and clinging to the belief that it does will lead to dissatisfaction and frustration.[ii]

Therefore, the road to happiness is one that doesn't end. It is a wonderful process and a journey. There are some people who are happier than you and some who are not as happy. That's how it will always be. When observing others, do not say, "Oh, he's happy, and she is not." There is really no such thing as *happy* or *unhappy*. There is only *happier*.

What Is Happiness?

"Happiness" is a term surprisingly difficult to define. Like beauty or truth, describing happiness remains a fun challenge for any aspiring philosopher. Really think about…what is happiness? Don't think about what causes happiness or what happiness does, but about what it is essentially. Probably any definition you came up with was something that caused happiness, such as friendship, freedom, or fulfilling work. These things can cause happiness, but they don't pass as a good working definition. Gas makes a car go, but you wouldn't say gas is a car. Perhaps your definition was a result of happiness, such as "a pep in my step" or a "smile on my face." Again, happiness will likely make you smile, but a smile isn't happiness. So, what is happiness, really? You will be strongly tempted to say, "Bah! I know it when I see it!" Though this idle definition will probably bring you closer to the truth, happiness has a good definition, and it's important to know.

Aristotle has the most widely accepted definition. He is the most important philosopher in Western thought, second only to the smartest man who ever lived—Jesus Christ. Three centuries before Jesus, he and his friends in Athens spent a great deal of time pondering big ideas, such as the meaning of life, virtue, and happiness. He was particularly famous for defining and categorizing important academic terms and disciplines we still use today, including biology, politics, psychology, and metaphysics. Here's his definition of happiness:

"The flourishing of the human soul."

Remember this definition. Happiness is not pleasure but a flourishing life that causes many wonderful things, including true pleasure. And, like a tree that never dies and can't stop growing, so this life, the flourishing one, is available to anyone.

Aristotle and his contemporaries believed virtue was the path to true happiness, the flourishing life. For the philosophers of ancient Greece, virtue was the goal, and happiness was the byproduct. This is important. They believed that if a person only pursued happiness as an ultimate goal (rather than as a byproduct of something more important, like virtue), he or she would inevitably stumble into a selfish and destructive life. What at first seems a harmless pursuit becomes a road to perdition. It becomes easy to use or hurt those around you to get what you want: happiness. This, of course, happens all the time.

According to Aristotle and his companions, not only does happiness come from virtue, but it specifically comes from four foundational virtues: prudence (acting with care or thought for the future); temperance (restraint and self-control); justice (the quality of being fair or reasonable); and courage (the ability to do something even though it scares you). At this point, the philosophers came close but didn't get it all right.

There are, of course, many other virtues—some more important than these four, that are more foundational to happy living. In essence, the ancient philosophers of Greece got the concept right. Happiness, the flourishing life, is the byproduct of making right choices and doing good. Though they are the most famous for this philosophical claim, they are not the oldest. King David said the same thing seven hundred years earlier.

The Translators' Choice (Blessed = Happy)

The Christian Bible is divided into two parts, the Old and New Testaments. The Old Testament was written in Hebrew, and the New Testament was written in Greek. If your Bible is written in English, a group of translators decided how to translate the words, sometimes making curious, and even incorrect, choices. In the end, something is always "lost in the translation," as they say.

One important example, which will serve our purpose, is the word "blessed." In the Bible, nearly every appearance of the word "blessed" can also be translated as "happy" (and, in fact, ought to be). The rule applies to both the Old and New Testaments.

So, the theme of happiness as a byproduct of a virtuous life is constant throughout the book of Psalms. It's most notably mentioned in the first psalm:

> How happy is the one who does not walk in the counsel of the wicked,
> Or stand in the way of sinners
> Or sit in the seat of mockers!
> But his delight is in the instruction of Jehovah
> And on His instruction he meditates day and night.
> He is like a tree planted by streams of water

Which yields its fruit in season
And whose leaf does not wither
Whatever he does prospers!

The psalmist is impressing upon the listener that happiness comes from a life of virtue bestowed on humankind by God's instruction. It's not just for a person who knows what is right and wrong, but also for someone who meditates day and night over what the Lord wants him or her to do. It's for a person who is passionate about living the right kind of life now. A person who does the right thing, not out of legalism, but out of shear delight in knowing he or she did the right thing is deeply happy.

David likens this person to a seed planted by a gentle stream. At first, it seems like nothing, but soon the seed grows into a huge tree that is lush with fruit, because it's firmly planted by the water. The tree abides near the water; therefore, it will always flourish. It doesn't happen overnight, but day in and day out, it is nourished by the water and eventually grows into something truly impressive.

The modern world doesn't support this concept. It's certainly not the message you get through ads on TV and the Internet. The modern world suggests that happiness and pleasure are equal, so that if you maximize pleasure and minimize pain, you will be happy. We observe *unhappy* people every day who have an abundance of things that ought to bring them pleasure and who simultaneously live a nearly pain-free existence, yet we still believe the myth. Pop culture conveys, "Get happiness, and get it now!" Sadly, this self-serving idea only leads to disenchantment and fractured, lonely lives. You cannot be both selfish and happy.

We Have an Inescapable Need to Be Good

Every single person has an innate, natural, need to be good. If a friend sat you down for an important talk and said, "Friend, you are not a happy person," this might cause you to be sad or perhaps reflective. You would wonder, looking at your own life, why you were not happy, or maybe you would think, *He doesn't understand.* It would probably stimulate quite a conversation.

But what if your friend said something different? What if he sat you down and said, "Friend, you are not a *good* person."? This would strike a much deeper chord. You would be visibly hurt or, at the very least, confused. You would think, *Someone must be gossiping,* or, *He misunderstands somehow.* Maybe you would even be angry. No matter what your response, you wouldn't be able to have much of a conversation, because you would insist that your friend simply misunderstands you. This is because everybody has an inescapable need to be good but only a desire to be happy. Even evil men are not likely to see themselves as evil, only misunderstood or, worse, truly good.

Happiness cannot exist in the life of the individual if she does not, at the very least, view herself as being good. This doesn't mean, in the short-term, that she has to actually be good, but she must at least think herself good. In the end, of course, if she is only fooling herself to maintain sanity and a semblance of happiness, her self-made house of cards will fall in on itself. In the words of author J. K. Rowling, "Darkness always turns in on itself." So, happiness cannot really exist without goodness. Therefore, if you want to be happy, pursue—with all your heart—a life of virtue and goodness.

Think about this. Rarely does a person, who knowingly does something wrong, say blatantly to everyone, "I know this is wrong, but I'm doing it anyway." When we do something we know is wrong, we do our best to rationalize why it's not a big deal. We seek the right friends to help us think it's OK, so we can proceed with a fooled conscience. Therefore, it's almost impossible for a person to say, "This is wrong, and this is right. I choose wrong." Instead, we have to say, "It's no big deal," for a person can't be both evil and happy. He must lie to himself or actually be good.

If God has blessed you with goodness and a happy life, don't throw away all you have by making a selfish mistake. G. K. Chesterton wrote in his masterpiece *Orthodoxy* that, "Happiness hangs on a veto." He likened it to fairy stories like Cinderella. Cinderella was given a coach, a beautiful dress, and a wonderful, unforgettable night. The only stipulation: she had to be home by midnight. Chesterton says:

> Also, she had a glass slipper; and it cannot be a coincidence that glass is so common a substance in folk-lore. This princess lives in a glass castle, that princess on a glass hill; this one sees all things in a mirror; they may all live in glass houses if they do not throw stones. For this thin glitter of glass everywhere is the expression of the fact that happiness is bright but brittle, like the substance most easily smashed by a maid or a cat…Strike glass, and it will not endure an instant; simply do not strike it, and it will endure a thousand years. Such, it seemed, was the joy of man, either in elfland or on earth.[iii]

Chesterton reminds us that, no matter how happy we are, our happiness can easily be undone by our conscience. Haunted by the ignoble and secret choices we make, happiness flees the selfish life with haste. The happy life is quickly shattered by a simple veto, a simple choice to cast it away in lieu of darker desires. The happiness of life cannot exist with selfishness, self-righteousness, meaninglessness, or an ongoing pattern of vice. Though it may not happen instantly, happiness will leave.

Virtue is the foundation of happiness. Virtue is the root of the tree. Virtue bears an undying fruit of joy, but perdition rots it away. This doesn't mean you must be perfect, but rather that you must seek right and not wrong. It's not just what you are but what you want to become. It's not having everything right all the time but the desire for right. Take comfort. You will always have a choice; that cannot be taken from you. If you choose right instead of wrong, you will be blessed with happiness.

So, in the end, a virtuous life and happy life walk hand in hand, like inseparable lovers. Happiness comes swiftly, when it is given away. When you truly help someone in need, at the cost of your own pleasure and comfort, happiness will inevitably flood your heart. When you grow in patience, self-control, peace, or in the control of your tongue, you will have built a firmer foundation upon which to build a happy existence.

If you thirst after God's will, even when it hurts, you are walking on the happy, narrow path of Christian living. Though it may take more than just doing the right thing sometimes, happiness cannot exist without goodness. Happiness is a by-product, a fruit born from the tree of right living. If you seek after happiness alone, you are likely to be disappointed. If you would only seek after goodness, the goodness taught by God in Christ Jesus, you will live both a good and happy life.

CHAPTER TWO

Acting Happy Glorifies God

"The glory of God is man fully alive."
—St. Iraneaus

It's Really OK to Be Happy

Growing up in the Schuller household, happiness was a matter of great importance and even intention. To Schullers, happiness was a choice, something you decided to have regardless of circumstance. Schullers can make anything positive, because we have overactive imaginations. Honestly, you should hear some of the positive spin my dad could come up with when I was a kid. If you said, "Ugh, I don't want to get out of bed today," he'd respond with, "It's better than the alternative!"

Every morning, I would wake to the sound of my dad's coffee grinder. He had this certain rhythm when he ground coffee. First, it was the solid grind, then, as the crunching sound went to a smooth flow, he would shake the grinder, giving it a wavy sound. Then you'd hear him smack it on the kitchen counter to get out the excess beans. At this point, I was already awake and knew what was coming next. He'd come up the stairs, whistling, on a mission to wake everybody up.

He always had different, creative ways of getting the kids out of bed, and you never knew how he was going to do it. One of his strategies was to quote a poem way too loudly, in an annoying, singsong tone:

> I'm going to be happy today
> Though the skies may be cloudy or gray
> No matter what may come my way
> I'm going to be happy today!

It was very likely that this song would be followed with scruffy, scratchy beard kissing that was enough to infuriate you into laughing, despite your anger, and to hopelessly flail your arms in defense. Slowly, I would crawl out of bed, not really feeling like facing a new day. I would come downstairs, eat Coach's Oats with everybody else, and head off to school with this poem stuck in my head—an earworm with my dad's voice as the lead singer. What I didn't know was that his parents used this famous poem from Ella Wheeler Wilcox on him and his sisters while they were growing up.

It makes sense that, in the end, this ritual embedded the Schuller value in my soul. It abides with me to this day. To a large degree, happiness is a choice, something we can have most of the time, regardless of what is happening around us. "I'm going to be happy today…" I'm glad I've believed that my whole life, because it has made me a happier, kinder, and more moral person.

I believe that happiness is a choice 90 percent of the time. I believe this, because there are always people who have less than I do who are happier than I am. There are people who have experienced more suffering and tragedy than I ever could, and they are happier than I am.

I once saw a child in Swaziland who hadn't eaten in two days. He had the biggest smile on his face. He was happy, because he was playing a fun game with rocks with his two brothers. Sure, he was hungry and didn't know where his next meal would come from, but he was happy. He had friends and a good game. His next meal came from me, which made me happy. Usually, the only thing keeping me from being happy is my own perspective, choosing to be stubborn and sour, forgetting all that I have.

My dad used to tell us another famous story. Once there were two twins who looked the same but had very different characters. One seemed to be happy all the time, no matter how bad things got, and one was unhappy all the time, no matter how good things got. Scientists were intrigued, so they decided to run a test in a laboratory. The details were always different every time he told the story, but the "scientists" version was always my favorite.

In my dad's story, the scientists set up two rooms. They filled one room with the coolest toys ever. They filled the other room with horse manure. They put the happy boy in the manure room and the unhappy boy in the toy room. When they checked the room with the unhappy boy, they thought, for sure, that he would be happy. After all, his room was a dream come true for any kid—there were all sorts of marvelous toys, video games, and some candy to boot. Of course, he was in a sour mood. There he was, sitting cross-legged in the middle of the room, weeping with frustration. When the scientists asked him why on earth he was crying, he replied, "Here you've got every toy in the whole world, but you forgot the one toy that was my favorite!" On and on, he continued to cry.

Then, they made their way to the manure room, where they were sure the other boy would be unhappy, if not traumatized, due to the stench of animal dung and refuse. To their surprise, the boy was laughing, jumping up and down, and flinging poo in the air.

Quickly, they opened the door and asked, "Son, what on earth are you doing?" With a breathless smile and a road apple in each hand, he said, "With all this pony poo, there's gotta be a pony in here somewhere!" Happiness. It's perspective, isn't it?

Most people were not as lucky as I was. Many people grow up in houses where being happy is frowned upon for one reason or another. Maybe it's a super-religious home where everyone believes happiness is bad. Perhaps it's a household where happiness is seen as silly, stupid, or unrealistic. It could even be a home where the mother or father is always in a fit, or is insensitive to those around them. No matter the reason, many of us have built patterns of unhappiness in our lives because of the way we grew up. Somehow, we came to believe that being happy most of the time was ridiculous and even immoral. This is not true. It's really OK to be happy almost all the time. In fact, it's better if you are.

When talking about happiness as a by-product of virtuous living, hitting the virtuous part over and again, we sometimes get confused. We may think that happiness is somehow immoral or that it's something we can have only when we have done everything perfectly in life and have behaved like moral paragons. This is not the case. Happiness is a wonderful thing, even if you are still making mistakes here and there. God wants us to have a happy, flourishing life in his kingdom. It's easy to see this scripturally, especially if one reads "happy" instead of "blessed" when studying the Bible.

Instead, we act as if happiness and joy have nothing to do with each other. People say things like, "Joy is 'all the time,' but happiness is a fleeting thing. Happiness just isn't enough." Sometimes you'd get the impression from preachers and biblical teachers that a person can have joy with a frown. There they are—reading their Bibles, sad and grumpy, with an Eeyore-like disposition and…joy, even though nobody can tell, including themselves. This is utter nonsense. Joy (the pervasive sense of well-being) and happiness (the flourishing of the human soul) go hand in hand. Joy is a celebration, a party-on the-inside coming from a wellspring of life—a knowledge that everything's going to be OK. Joy is total surrender and trust in God that results in a big, toothy smile. It is part and parcel of God's plan for us. A smile is a holy thing.

God wants us to be happy, because he is the happiest, most joy-filled being in the universe. He takes incredible pleasure and delight in his creation. American philosopher and theologian, Dallas Willard says, "We should…think God leads a very interesting life, and that His life is full of joy."[iv] There are places on earth that would take your breath away, if you could only see them. God sees them every day!

Yosemite is perhaps the most beautiful place on earth. It's called "God's playground," and for good reason. I will always cherish the memory of the first time my eyes fell on the valley in Yosemite. Waterfalls poured off giant cliffs into mirror-like lakes and rivers filled with gold flakes. Meadows there are filled with yellow flowers and crowned with giant sequoias.

God is in Yosemite right now. He's also with you as you read this. God is everything that it means to be filled with light and life, total mirth, joy, and creativity. God is a fullness and a wellspring. He is the happiest being in the universe. Every day, we wake up in the presence of God's joy and happiness at having us as **his** children. He wants us to be like **him**: happy, celebrating life.

Being Happy Is Godly and Altruistic

I was scanning AM radio, trying to find the Angels baseball game, when I heard a voice say one of the most interesting things I've ever heard: "Welcome to *The Happiness Hour*, where every day I remind you that happy people make the world a better place, and unhappy people make it a worse place. Acting happy is altruistic." It was *The Happiness Hour*, on the *Dennis Prager Radio Show*.

This man, who is typically very political, devotes an entire hour every Friday to a discussion with his listeners about the theory of happiness. No politics are allowed. People call in and dialogue with him every week on the issue of happiness. His overarching thesis is that happy people make the world a better place. He believes that people should work on being happy for the benefit of others. In other words, acting happy is a good deed!

The words I mention above honestly shocked me when I first heard them, but the more I listened, the more I could see they were true. Prager gave so many wonderful examples. Happy people make the world a better place, because they lift people up and encourage people when they are feeling down. Happy people are always reminding people of the simple blessings of life. Unhappy people make others feel that they ought not be happy around them.

Unhappy people have lots of reasons why those around them shouldn't be happy and are quick to share them. All you have to do is ask someone with an unhappy spouse, parents, children, or coworkers if acting happy around others is a kindness, an act of altruism. Some people would do anything if they could just see their unhappy loved ones be happy for a single day, a single hour. Happy people give more to charity and volunteer more.

When you think of the worst villains in history, it's impossible to imagine them as happy people. They are always unhappy people who hurt because of their unhappiness. Prager helped me realize that I ought to work on being happy, because my happiness is a blessing to others! It enriches and encourages those who live and work with me. Acting happy is a good deed.

Prager, who teaches at the local Jewish seminary,

probably got some of his ideas from the great Rabbi Nachman of Breslov. Rabbi Nachman, who lived and taught in eighteenth-century Ukraine, had thousands of followers and impacted the way many Jews interpret the Bible. He was a mystic who believed we could have constant communion with God and be filled with true joy. Rabbis like Nachman give a great deal of attention to the term "mitzvah," which is a holy commandment from God.

Rabbi Nachman's main teaching was, "It is a great mitzvah to be happy always!" He believed that God not only wanted people to be happy but that he also commanded them to be happy! He thought acting happy shouldn't be based on your emotions but rather a principled dedication to obeying God's command: "Act happy." He thought acting happy, even when you didn't feel happy, was the right thing to do morally.

Here are some of his reflections on being as happy as possible, as often as possible:

- Make every effort to maintain a happy, positive outlook at all times. It is a natural human tendency to become discouraged and depressed because of the hardships of life; everyone has their full share of suffering. That is why you must force yourself to be happy at all times. Use every possible way to bring yourself to joy, even by joking or acting a little crazy!

- If you are happy, the whole world benefits.

• Even if you are upset and unhappy, you can at least put on a happy front. At first, you may not feel genuinely happy in your heart. Even so, if you act happy, you will eventually attain true happiness and joy.

This last point from Rabbi Nachman is the hardest one for us to swallow. He taught and believed that even if you weren't happy, you should act and even pretend to be happy around other people. It blesses their lives. He also believed that, if you act or pretend to be happy, this pretense would actually become a reality. He went so far as to presume that acting unhappy, especially when you had little reason, was an act of selfishness that was inconsiderate to those around you.

Rabbi Nachman's reflections can feel shocking, or even offensive, but that doesn't mean he's wrong. Nachman stumbled on something that could bring a great deal of happiness to people: the belief that emotions won't dictate actions. If one feels discouraged, one should still act encouraging. If one is suffering, one should alleviate the suffering of others with a smile. If one feels angry, one should act mercifully to those around him or her.

Emotions greatly influence the decisions we make, but they do not have the last word on our conduct. We can control and train our emotions. Acting happy is possible, even when we don't feel emotions that typically coincide with happiness. Nachman believed something radical: instead of allowing our emotions to dictate our actions, our actions can dictate our emotions. He was right.

"Fake It Till You Make It"

The idea of being fake or phony is displeasing to many of us. But, there is real evidence that acting happy, even when you don't feel happy, causes you to feel happier in the long run. This method is often used to help people who are struggling with depression or addiction. In the twelve-step program, the catch phrase is "fake it till you make it."

Cognitive behavioral therapists use the same method. If an individual pretends to be happy by doing all the things happy people do, that person will then typically feel happy. If he fake-smiles, often real laughter follows. It changes the way he thinks, as a happy outlook becomes his self-fulfilling prophecy. Act happy, even when you don't feel happy, and you'll become a happier person.

Many people say they can't act happy when they don't feel happy. Rubbish. In the words of J. P. Moreland, "Feelings make wonderful slaves but terrible masters." It is important not to allow emotions and feelings to always dictate our choices. Rather, our choices should pave the way for what kind of feelings we have. We should act happy. We do things like this all the time.

You can just see the image in your head of a woman yelling at her husband, and then the phone rings. With a charming voice, and maybe even a smile, she answers, "Doe residence; this is Jane." Here she is, acting happy with a stranger but unhappy with the person who wants her happiness more than anything.

Once, a friend of mine was at a baseball game, and a decorated young soldier came up to the beer stand where he was waiting to get a drink. He told me he didn't have any feelings of love or blessing for this guy, but felt that buying him a beer at a ball game was just the right thing to do. After treating the soldier to a beer and saying "thank you for your service," he said he noticed deep feelings of gratitude and brotherly love toward the soldier, almost like a burning in his chest.

Notice, he didn't commit this act of kindness for the soldier because of feelings he had on the inside; he did it on principle. The wonderful feelings followed his choice. If you want to be a happy person, and you want to bless the people who live and work with you, act happy today, and you will be happy tomorrow!

Acting Happy Is an Act of Faith

One exception to all this is tragedy. I hope it's obvious that in the midst of tragedy you ought to allow yourself to mourn instead of acting happy. The idea of being happy when something terrible happens is unkind and not God's plan for us. I wouldn't like my wife to be happy if I were to die or be seriously injured. In fact, her sadness and tears demonstrate how much she loved me. But, in the end, I would still want her to learn what it means to be happy without me.

For those of you who have lost loved ones, the most important question for you to ask is not "Why are they dead?" but rather, "Why am I still alive?" You may ask yourself what your loved ones expect of you now. If they love you, they expect and hope that you will lead a happy and flourishing life.

Here are some reflections and some guiding principles for acting happy:

First, many of us are going to be unhappy unless something makes us happy. So, we sit around or journey through life hoping something, or someone, will come along and make us happy. The default, then, is unhappiness: "I will be unhappy unless something makes me happy." Instead, it is better that we decide to be happy as our default: "I will be happy unless something makes me unhappy." Therefore, the default is happiness. Every morning, we will wake up with the decision to act happy, for the benefit of others and ourselves, unless something horrible happens. Then, we no longer look to the things on the outside to magically make us feel something like happiness.

Prager has another interesting thought: unhappiness is easy. It requires little work or effort. It is something for which you can blame others as you wallow in misery. It's the lazy man's game. Unhappy people often chew on their gloom like a hamburger. It's a part of their identity, and they're not about to give it up.

Happiness, on the other hand, is the work of champions. It requires real work and dedication. It means focusing on the things you ought to focus on. Happiness is something earned through dedication, prayer, good deeds, and the formation of new healthy patterns. Though happiness is harder for some than it is for others, it always requires effort, reflection, and perseverance.

Finally, acting happy is an act of faith. This is why belief in God is so important in the journey toward true happiness. As a follower of Jesus, I trust that he treasures me and has my best interests in mind. I know he looks at me with more love, care, and affection than I have for my own kids. This is almost impossible to comprehend, but it gives me confidence. He has my well-being in mind.

I know that someday, no matter what happens, I will be in his eternal care. So, even when things are not the way I want them to be, acting happy in the midst of hardship is an act of faith. It's my way of showing God that I trust him and believe that he has the last word.

Therefore, my happiness is something I share with God. I am happy, because God is happy and wants me to be happy with him. I am filled with joy in partnership with God. I know that all the good things I have in life come from him, and I live a life of gratitude and joy, knowing the best is always yet to come. No matter how good it gets, it's always going to get even better!

Choose happiness. Understand that people in your life want you to be happy. God wants you to be happy. This does not mean being selfish or seeking pleasure, but it does mean living with a smile on your face. St. Iraneaus said, "The glory of God is man fully alive." There is almost no better witness to your faith than acting happy. It is altruistic to act happy around the people who are closest to you. It is a good deed to act happy with your coworkers. It is a blessing to everyone for you to add a little more laughter and mirth to the world. Acting happy is your duty. Becoming happy is your reward.

CHAPTER THREE

Happy While Suffering

"Be as a bird perched on a frail branch, that she
feels bending beneath her, still she sings away all
the same, knowing she has wings to fly."
—Victor Hugo

Happy Are Those Who Suffer

I just held a funeral for a man who died of cancer
in prison. He was one of the happiest people I knew,
even though, by all standards, he shouldn't have been.
More than likely, he was falsely accused. He passed two
lie detector tests with flying colors. He had no back-
ground of crime or misconduct, and yet he was stuck
with a twenty-year sentence. He and his wife sold

everything they had to fight the case and still lost. His kids would continue to grow up without him. His wife would struggle every day for money, as he was stuck behind bars.

I would have gone mad. I would have been angry with God and everyone else. He wasn't. The most important question we can ask (we who still have our freedom, families, and good names) is why? How could someone who should be in the midst of terrible suffering still be happy? The answer: he found meaning in his struggle.

Every day, he would draw pictures of stories in the Bible. Before he went to prison, he didn't have much faith, but after his imprisonment, he hung all sorts of illustrations of Bible stories and wonderfully written prayers from his cell wall. Everyone in the prison knew he was the guy to go to for wisdom and prayer. He was an encourager and always helped everyone see the bright side, the silver lining.

One person he knew there was released from prison and spoke at his funeral; he said he was the nicest and happiest person he ever knew. Everyone wanted to be around him when they were having a tough day. In the darkness, light always shines brighter. He was able to illuminate the dark places. He found meaning and purpose because he believed he was in God's care. He took Jesus's words seriously when he said, "You are the light of the world." How could someone, in the midst of such an awful situation, still be a glowing example of happiness and encouragement? He was more than blessed. He was happy.

Again, in most places in the Bible, the term "blessed" can also be interpreted as "happy." The place where this seems to make the least amount of sense is Jesus's important and famous discourse, The Sermon on the Mount and the opening Beatitudes.[vi] Here we remember Jesus's words: "Blessed are the poor in spirit." Traditionally, many pastors and priests teach the Beatitudes as a type of moral list, like the Ten Commandments. They would say Jesus is explaining the goodness of being meek, poor in spirit, in mourning, and so on. But this is not at all what Jesus was getting at.

He was standing at the bottom of a hill that rose up like a Greek amphitheater, with thousands of suffering people sitting upon it, as though they were having a picnic. Many of the people followed Jesus because they wanted him to solve their problems and aid them in their suffering. Sick and wounded people, hungry kids, and people who had been robbed or falsely accused all sat on that hill before Jesus. There were guilty people, wealthy people, poor people, religious people, hookers, and thieves. Most of the people there wanted some miracle or oracle from Jesus. They were patiently waiting for him to get through his sermon so they could get what they wanted. And so he began the greatest sermon that has ever been preached—he began with the Beatitudes.

These Beatitudes were not lessons on how to live moral lives, but rather a proclamation that everyone who suffers is now really happy because the kingdom of heaven has now come to earth in Jesus Christ. Being "poor in spirit," for example, is a terrible thing. It means to be spiritually bankrupt and without a spiritual bone in your body. It doesn't mean "being a humble person."

He was speaking to all the people who thought they weren't religious or spiritual enough to know God or be a part of a church (synagogue). He was coming to change the way they viewed God and suffering. Therefore, the Beatitudes in Matthew 5:3–9 should be interpreted very differently than the way most churches interpret them. "Blessed are the meek" should be read to the effect of, "Happy are the doormats." "Blessed are those who hunger and thirst for righteousness" should be read to the effect of, "Happy are those who deserve justice and haven't had it." This part refers to someone who has been violated in some way by someone who has gotten away with it. This section does not refer to someone who desires to be a righteous person.

In summary, all eight Beatitudes are different modes of suffering, not commandments. Jesus is saying that happiness is coming to those who are suffering, because he has come with his kingdom. He is saying that anyone can be happy now in Christ, because he is bringing something better and bigger that will outshine everything they've lost. How? By turning suffering, hurting people into the light of the world and the salt of the earth. By bathing these people in meaning and joy, the kind that can only come from following Jesus. By using the most hurt and broken people to make the biggest impact the world has ever seen.

Those famous lines come right after the Beatitudes. Jesus tells the hurting and suffering people around him that happiness has come upon them because they are going to live a new kind of life that will bring light and life to the dark world they live in. Jesus calls them to rise above the hurt and anger and become a new kind of person who will be a hero or champion for God.

This kind of person will live from a deeper center that flourishes from the Spirit, imputed into the heart of those who believe in Jesus. They will have an eternal kind of living that will begin right now, if only they trust and believe. He will call on them, just like he called my friend in prison, to be encouraging, loving, praying, persevering, gracious, and unworried illuminators. He is calling them to shine with selfless commitment to something bigger than their current trials. He's calling them to a meaningful life.

Living life with Jesus doesn't mean living a perfect life without suffering if only you have enough faith. Eternal living with Jesus means that no trial or tribulation can pull you away from the sustaining power that comes from knowing your calling. Jesus says to these people on the hill, "You are the light of the world. You are the salt of the earth!" In my understanding of Christian doctrine and other things Jesus has said in the gospels, I might have thought Jesus would have said, "I, Jesus Christ, am the light of the world," but he didn't! He said, "You are."

He starts the light within us, but we are his plan for illuminating a dark world. He is counting on us to rise above the muck and mire of our lives for the benefit of others. He is calling us to something huge, the thing we were born to be and do, and that's something to be very happy and excited about!

Don't Fear Suffering

Don't live life in fear of pain or suffering. The fear of suffering causes more unhappiness than the suffering itself. This is one of the great ironies in the study of happy living. Many live in an abyss of daily worry and indecision because of their fear of suffering or pain that could possibly result from making big decisions or taking risks. Men carry on in relationships for years without proposing because of the fear of being stuck in a bad marriage or losing the adventure of being with other women. Parents smother their children with all sorts of nonsense in the hope that they'll live risk-free lives, sabotaging their childhood in the process.

Too often, trips are not taken, phone calls are not made, jobs are not applied for, and businesses are not started because of the fear of what might happen if something goes wrong. How many men would be happier if they just had the guts to ask a certain girl for her phone number?

My wife, Hannah, got a new car when she turned sixteen and kept it in perfect shape for two years. She eventually realized that it didn't have a scratch on it and became paranoid. That day, she got into her first fender-bender, and she's convinced, to this day, that it happened because of her worry. Suffering and pain will happen. Don't worry. Deal with it as it comes.

There really isn't anything in this world that leads to happiness that doesn't involve some kind of pain or suffering. Living and suffering go hand in hand. To go through life without suffering or pain is to go through life without risk or living. That life is numb. Of course, the numbness many of us deal with every day is a form of suffering in its own right. Life requires pain and risk for it to mean anything at all.

Recently, Hannah and I returned home from the hospital with our second child, a beautiful baby boy weighing eight pounds and twelve ounces and totally healthy. We couldn't ask for anything more than to know he is healthy, that my wife Hannah is healthy, and that our family is now larger by one. It's a thrill to know that God has trusted us with the care of raising one of his children. Today, our new son is the greatest source of happiness and meaning in our lives.

Conversely, he is an incredible challenge, as all new

babies are. He wants to be held constantly. If you put on your favorite shirt or jacket, fresh from the dry cleaners, he is guaranteed to spit up on it. But the worst is that Hannah and I hardly sleep at all. I tell people it's more like a chain of short naps than a good night's sleep. Every day at home, we're overly distracted by the chaos of young children, and every day at the office, I'm bogged down by my tiredness from lack of sleep. Today, our son is the greatest source of suffering and fatigue in our lives.

Here is the most surprising thing of all: at this moment, my greatest source of happiness is also my greatest source of suffering! We can't choose either. If we want the happiness of being parents, we must also endure the struggle of raising a child. Through this needed suffering, the whole family grows spiritually and bonds in ways that can only come through struggle. This metaphor applies to every life. Meaning rarely comes without suffering, and suffering rarely comes without meaning.

Why Does God Let Me Suffer?

Love is the reason we suffer. That's the short answer to this old and tired question. God created all people in his image to commune with them and experience real love with them. If love is to be real, it must also include choice. This is the most important thing to remember. For us to truly love God, we must have the ability to choose to move toward or away from him.

For the love between you and God to be real, there must always be a tree from which you may pluck "freedom from God" and devour it entirely. He did not make us like robots, programmed to do what he wants. He made people. He made us with choice, so our love is real. If I point a gun at my wife and tell her to kiss me, is that kiss real? If I offer her some amount of money to kiss me, is that kiss real? No, a kiss requires choice and desire.

The decisions we make to sin and hurt people are choices that go against God. God will not take away your choice or your ability to harm those who are near you, even the innocent ones. He will not program us to do the right thing, even though there is a risk that we may harm others. Many people do.

Spiritually, we say this "going away from God" invited some pretty dark things into our world. The more people choose to walk away from God, the darker our world becomes. The more people choose to be loving, selfless, peaceful, and godly, the lighter and better our world becomes. Think of candles in a dark room. The more candles there are, the more light.

Why Is God Invisible?

Imagine if God were to simply confront us more directly. Imagine a crude, Hollywood-like opening of the sky. God pokes his head through and says, "Hello, world! It's me, God. Just wanted to let you know I exist." Then, he tips his hat and vanishes. If this happened, people who don't want God in their lives will be forced to have him, whether they want him or not. In this scenario, our choice disappears. The ideas of heaven and hell now are inescapable, undeniable realities. In this impossible scenario, God is a tyrant rather than a robot programmer.

Saying that a person has reformed his life after visibly seeing God is like saying a thief caught in the act of stealing jewelry has changed his ways because he put the diamond back. The thief never would have returned the diamond without the cop's threat. God wants people to love the good. He wants people to do the right thing, not because of fear of punishment, but because it's the best way to live life. He wants people to have the freedom to choose their own way—to walk away from him or to hate him and deny his existence. It must be this way, for the sake of love and morality.

Sometimes we suffer because of natural disasters. Sometimes we suffer, because people harm us. But other times we suffer because, in the end, it was a part of God's plan for a better life. I say this with caution. It's rare that God lets us suffer in order to teach us something. Still, some suffering helps us grow, to the point that we may look upon it one day with fondness.

I'll never forget learning how to ride my bicycle. My dad offered me five dollars if I would let him take my training wheels off and give it a go with two wheels only. There we were, at the end of our cul-de-sac. My dad had his hand on my back. We were moving fast and without training wheels, and, at some point, he gently released me, and I didn't even feel it. Glancing back, I noticed he was fifteen feet behind me, and, out of fear, I began to wobble and crashed.

There I was, crying with a skinned knee. I was terribly upset at my dad for letting go of the bike. I was crying, shouting in anger. He cradled me in a way that embarrassed and bothered me. "Let go," I heaved away in anger, without understanding him. Eventually, I got back on and learned to ride without my dad but not without a little pain and struggle.

Allow me to ask the question: was it wrong of my dad to let me go? Did he do it with the malicious intention of harming me? Should he have continued to hold onto my bike for all these years? Imagine that. Here I am, a grown man with a family, and my wife asks to go on a bike ride. There we are, going down the boardwalk on our bikes, my dad striding alongside, with his hand on my back. There we are, having a romantic bike ride—just the three of us. That's silly. We sometimes forget that God is our Father. God is deeply concerned with our growth and maturity. Sometimes we suffer or endure pain, so that we will grow stronger and learn more. This is not always the case. I don't think God causes tragedy in our lives to help us grow (although we can grow through it). But please remember, especially when facing finances, bad breakups, job loss, or other temporary troubles, that God may be stretching and growing you into a better person.

D = S − M (Despair = Suffering − Meaning)

Viktor Frankl was the greatest person in my lifetime to understand and write about suffering. He had a huge impact on psychology and religion, influencing many great thinkers, including my grandfather. Frankl was a Jewish neurologist and psychologist who led a long, nightmarish existence in the bowels of Nazi concentration camps. Unlike many of the survivor stories we hear, Frankl's is unique, because he used his experience as a case study for human nature.

Life in the concentration camps disproved many of the theories of human nature he'd studied at the university. For example, Freud believed that if you broke people down to the bare-bones minimum in a place of fear, nakedness, and despair, they would all turn to ravenous wolves. But Frankl saw that this was only true sometimes. Many of the prisoners gave up food or other valuable items to their neighbors, even though they themselves were suffering terribly. Some people would even make jokes and cheer others up, even though they themselves ought to have been angry and distraught.

Frankl realized the most important thing in our lives is to discover life's meaning: the meaning of its beauty, experiences, work, and even suffering. Frankl believed that living from a place of meaning could give the individual the power to get through any ordeal. He realized despair was not the result of suffering but rather the result of suffering without meaning. This is true for all humans, whether they're in a concentration camp or not.

Frankl created an easy-to-remember formula that operated, in large part, as the thesis of his career. $D = S - M$, or rather Despair = Suffering without Meaning.[vii] The gloomy desolation of our souls does not come from hardship, suffering, pain, or bad circumstances. Rather, our misery results from experiencing these things without understanding their meaning.

Frankl believed that every experience of suffering had a deeper meaning that was waiting to be discovered. Every individual on an arduous path must know where his or her path leads and why it goes the way it does. It is of primal and paramount concern that we know the deeper meaning of every awful human experience. Only then can our suffering build us up instead of tearing us down.

According to Frankl's notions, suffering on any level fell into one of three categories he called "the Triad of Suffering." He wrote some wonderful reflections about how we can respond to suffering when it comes in any of these three forms. Here are some of his ideas in my own words along with some personal reflections. The three types of human suffering are: pain, guilt, and change.

The Triad of Suffering

Pain

Many of us imagine pain when we think of suffering, and for good reason. We go through many forms of pain: physical ailments, loss of homes and resources, or hunger. Pain is something we try desperately to control, avoid, and find relief from. How much money do pharmaceutical companies make helping people alleviate their pain?

Pain, in itself, is a terrible thing, and I pray that everyone who suffers from pain will be relieved. However, in this world, some of us are stuck with suffering and pain and don't see any real light at the end of the tunnel. We know loved ones who are constantly in pain and pray for them often. How do we respond to this? Can we be happy even though our life is painful? The answer is yes.

First, don't lose hope. Many believe they will never find relief from their pain. Hang in there, one day at a time. I have seen, time and again, people with ailments so serious that they should have died or would leave them in the grip of constant, chronic pain. Some of these people, however, have overcome their pain. Some thought they were trapped, but then doctors discovered a new procedure. Some were misdiagnosed. Other times, God has blessed them with an outright miracle.

My wife's grandmother was miraculously healed of an inoperable cancer. She continued to live life cancer-free for more than seven years. Eventually she had a relapse that quickly took her life. She wasn't healed in the second instance, but she was grateful to have been given such a wonderful gift of healing and seven pain-free years. We live in a strange world, and there are many things we don't understand. Still, we must never, ever, ever give up hope. Giving up hope may be giving up your miracle!

Still, what do we do with today's pain—not just sickness, but all types of pain? When Frankl was in the concentration camp, he realized he was completely powerless as he faced the unjust torment of injury, hunger, cold, and exhaustion that a brutal police state had inflicted upon him. He noted everything had been taken from him: his clothing, his treasures, his food, and even his wife. But he realized there was something that could never be taken from him: his ability to choose how to respond to his suffering. No matter what, they could not force him to be cruel, to wallow, or to develop a negative attitude.

The fact that his choice was always his own gave him a tremendous sense of power. He saw how many who were imprisoned with him also used this ability to choose to bless others with a treasured crust of bread, a cigarette, or a funny joke. No one can tell you how to respond to your pain; no one can take away your choice. How, then, should we see our pain? Like all suffering, we should see it as our greatest teacher by allowing it to develop our inner selves. Eventually, our pain will teach us to transcend it with humor and heroism.

There is something about pain that can reveal your true self. Pain can bring out the worst—or the best—in a person. It's amazing how pain can cause the nicest person to become angry, self-loathing, and toxic, or the most hurried, selfish person to become kind, reflective, and giving. Pain changes a person, for better or worse. It's strange and magic in a way—unpredictable. What does pain do to you when it comes at the worst time? How do you choose to respond?

Frankl believed the human soul was like a Roman arch. Rome was an amazing and brilliant civilization that revealed its intellect through engineering. The most famous Roman masterpiece of engineering, still visible all over the world, is the Roman arch. Arches, if they have been unmolested by history, continue to stand today, all over Europe and the Middle East. Frankl said he was surprised when he heard about the manner in which ancient arches are repaired. He said that when the stones become loose and the grouting becomes old, they don't take the arch apart and put it back together. They simply add more weight. When they do this, everything pushes closer together, and the arch becomes much stronger, ready to face another thousand years of wear and tear.

He said the human being is like this. You might think that putting suffering upon the shoulders of a man will make him weaker, but it will likely make him stronger and prepare him for the rest of what life is going to throw at him. Man has an incredible ability to allow pain to be his teacher. Though it is shocking and uncomfortable at first, pain can reveal things about us that we've never understood: things about our families, the choices we've made, or deep wounds of the heart we never knew existed.

Pain in any form also gives us the opportunity to live in solidarity with those who are suffering more than we are. When this happens, an individual can find a new purpose, a crusade to end the suffering of all people with ailments similar to his or her own. Many times, successful people are inflicted with strange illnesses and start foundations or fund research grants to end the affliction of others. It's not that these people were selfish before; that particular affliction simply wasn't on their radar.

It isn't just the wealthy who do this. A member of my church suffers from terrible back pain as a result of falling from a ladder. He went through a very dark time and had to rearrange his life to accommodate constant pain and his new difficulty with walking. He didn't allow the pain to conquer his life. Rather, he wanted to find a way to bring meaning to his suffering.

So, he started the main outreach to the local elderly retirement home. He is perfectly suited for the job, because he understands the needs of the people who suffer with pain or struggle to walk. He is always prepared. He has the right van, the right equipment, and a sensitivity that makes those he cares for feel loved and understood.

Did God cause his pain so he could do this? No, I really don't think so. But God did build him up. God helped him make an important decision. This man decided he wouldn't let his ailment poison the treasure of living life to the fullest. He transcended his own pain by helping those in need.

Another friend of mine broke his back in a snowboarding accident and struggled for years with terrible pain in his leg. For twenty years, he had to take morphine and other drugs just to get on with his day-to-day living. Over time, the pain helped him rethink the way he was living life, and he became closer to God and his family as a result. One day, he was having a conversation with a friend of a friend who happened to be a spine doctor. They eventually started talking about his back injury, and the doctor said, "I think I can fix that!"

This doctor specialized in the exact problem my friend had and was able to repair his spine with a new procedure that had only been developed recently. Even though my friend suffered so much, he never gave up hope, and his suffering helped him to grow. Now, he has to face a different kind of challenge: he has to wean himself from the pain medication. Here again is a different kind of suffering through pain, but I know that he will allow God to show him the meaning within this new struggle, and he will beat it.

What a challenge to change the way we view life when we are being physically taxed with pain we don't deserve! We cannot let the pain win, even when we can't change or undo it. We must understand that this pain can't take away our ability to choose how we'll respond. Even when there really is no hope for relief, we must allow the pain and suffering to be our greatest teacher.

The two best ways to change our mind-set in the midst of pain are heroism and humor. The examples above are about people who allowed their pain to bring them into new ways of viewing the world. They transcended their own pain by living like Christ and helping others who were suffering more. This is heroism: helping others at your own cost.

The second tool is humor. God made the human spirit in such a way that it could laugh, even in the worst of circumstances. In college, I was in a friendly dorm room wrestling match with a giant Hawaiian friend. He was twice my weight and three times stronger, and yet, stupidly, I thought I might have a chance. Somewhere, after body slamming me, he jumped higher than I had thought possible for a man his size, and landed square on my chest. It hurt.

At first I thought I might have broken a rib, but it was just some bruising. The doctor told me I just needed to get some rest and not to laugh too much.

The very idea got me laughing, right there in the doctor's office. Of course, this led to a torturous, and yet humorous, couple of weeks. Every time I laughed it hurt, but this was funny in and of itself. Of course, my unhelpful friends, even the guilty Hawaiian, found a new hobby: doing whatever they could to make me laugh to make me writhe in pain. Those were some of the best weeks ever, and I wouldn't trade them for the world.

On more than one occasion, I have visited a man on his deathbed who was cracking jokes. Everyone around him was sad and weepy, and there he was telling jokes about the grim reaper and buying the farm. Everyone was hurting, and he was the one doing the comforting and the uplifting. He's the one dying! That is a good kind of person. This is the kind of person who doesn't allow pain, suffering, or even death to poison any moment of life, which is a gift from God. Though there are times when mourning and sadness should be our mode, being a humorous and encouraging person in the midst of pain is a truly wonderful thing.

Guilt

Few things in this world are as awful as gnawing guilt: knowing you have done something wrong and keeping it secret. This is, of course, what we do with guilt. We humans are so terrified of confessing and reforming our ways that we bury the guilt deep down inside and allow it to burrow deeper. When this happens, we become different people, quick to anger, legalistic, hurried, and addicted.

One of the primary teachings of the Christian faith is how to deal with guilt. The crucifixion and resurrection of Christ are inseparable events that signify, in the life of those who believe, total forgiveness and renewal. We believe that all people have sinned and everyone falls short of the perfection of God's glory. Because of this, God has offered the whole world a chance to be completely forgiven of everything and to be restored to his family. There is nothing we can do to earn this forgiveness. It's a free gift of love from God to us, freeing us from the suffering that comes from guilt.

If we allow this forgiveness to permeate our being, it will heal a deep wound and change us. From a new place of love and forgiveness, we are free to love and forgive others in the same way God has forgiven us in Christ Jesus. We don't judge others because they sin differently than we do. We begin to see all people the way God sees them, with love and optimism.

Though we cannot do anything to earn this forgiveness, God expects two things from us in return, both of which require courage and effort. The first is public confession, and the second is reform.

The most difficult thing to do, when you've made a mistake secretly, is to confess it to someone you respect and love. After all, your confession may cost you your reputation and friendship. To confess your mistakes publicly does not mean announcing your mistakes at work, at church, or to everyone on the Internet. Good confession means going either to the person you hurt or to one or two mature people so that they may forgive you, pray for you, and be a manifestation of God's restoration to you. They can be like Christ to you, helping lift the burden of secret sin from your shoulders. You can take off the heavy mask of pretense and just be you, wounded and ready to receive their love and forgiveness.

Guilt is like a wound. It is much better when it is on the outside. Imagine you are a doctor in an emergency room, and two patients come in who have both been wounded in a car accident. One patient has cuts, wounds, blood, and injured skin on the outside—a repulsive sight, but he has no serious internal injuries. The other patient is fine on the outside—no cuts or blood, but he is hemorrhaging on the inside. Which one is in better shape? Obviously, the one who is wounded on the outside! This is because all the vital organs are on the inside. On the outside, the doctor can apply bandages and medicine, but when the wound is internal, it is much more dangerous.

Secret guilt is a wound on the inside, but confession brings the wound to the outside and allows the doctor to heal it. You carry the pain deep within. It is killing you, yet you pretend like you're all right. Everybody probably knows you're not. Confess and be healed. How many times have you needlessly carried the burden of secret guilt only to find the terrible weight of shame removed upon the bright day of your confession?

What a happy day it will be when you no longer have to wear a mask and pretend. What a great day when you can stop lying and hiding. From a place of forgiveness and public confession, it is time to walk the happy road of reform.

Become a different kind of person, a Jesus kind of person. I like penance. It used to be that people who confessed their sins were given some sort of task to perform to train them into new patterns of living. Though historically there have been some serious problems with people thinking they can earn forgiveness by doing penance, I still love the idea of doing something as a form of training yourself into goodness. If you have made a big mistake, it's time to do something to make it up.

This requires reflection and prayer, but ask that God give you some kind of task to train your body into Christian behavior. If you stole, spend some time volunteering at a homeless shelter. If you blew up in anger at someone, do some kind of work of love, like giving him or her a gift and writing a note of apology. If you've stumbled into pornography, give up your computer, cell phone, or TV for a month. Go on pilgrimages. Fast. Make anonymous donations to charity. Pray for others. Get a vision for the kind of person God wants you to be, and reform your life.

By doing this, even guilt becomes meaningful, as we allow it to be our teacher, changing us into good people. For more information on reforming your life after the image of Christ, read the most important book written in my lifetime: *The Divine Conspiracy* by Dallas Willard.[viii]

Change

The third, and sometimes most difficult, form of suffering is change. Suffering from change comes in many forms: the loss of a church, a bad breakup or divorce, getting fired or laid off, graduating from school and going out into the working world, death, living life without a good friend or spouse. The world we live in constantly changes, and this is the source of so much suffering.

Everything, even the smallest molecule, is changing and in constant flux. People come and people go. Organizations, businesses, even nations rise and fall, and we have to suffer through it all. How do we deal with this change? How can we cope with a new life without our spouse? How can we go on when all our work has been destroyed? How can we have fun when all our friends have moved to different places? How can we live when all our children have left our home, making it feel empty? Change causes such a great amount of pain.

It is true that sometimes these changes bring new opportunities. For example, empty nester couples often experience a short period of pain, but they end up having a better marriage in the end. Though they have to deal with change in the family, they have more time for each other. Obviously, we want to find the bright side of change and look for new, exciting opportunities. However, I want to focus on what we do when the opportunities have not yet revealed themselves. How do we cope?

We find strength in the midst of change with this important knowledge: the past is eternal and unchanged. Every event in life has meaning, because it cannot stand independent from the world. Everything you do in life, from ordering tacos to sending e-mails, has an effect on eternity. It's like dropping a stone in a large lake. The ripples seem to go on forever.

In the same way, every good thing you have done in your life will continue to affect the whole world, even after you're gone. This may seem insignificant, but every life is important, because every decision you make impacts others. Students of chaos theory often say things like, "The flap of butterfly wings in Washington, under the right conditions, is enough to cause a tornado in Texas." This means history is the ongoing story resulting from the choices people have made even thousands of years ago.

Every choice you make matters. And the choices you make today will affect the world tomorrow. It could be that Joseph Stalin was the result of one unkind thing a man said to his brother three hundred years earlier. It could be that Mother Teresa was the result of one child's selfless act of love toward a homeless woman a thousand years before.

We have no idea how our choices will affect future generations. This is a great hope in a world that is constantly changing. It means you have left your mark on the world just by existing. Everything in the past has already happened and is fixed in history. That is one thing that cannot be changed or undone. What kind of history will you make today? Never forget: your choices matter.

My grandparents are well known in the world of ministry. They created a local congregation that became a television church to millions. They inspired hope and healing for a sea of people all around the world. At one time, this ministry thrived and was at the forefront of outreach. Many people saw it as an example of great success in ministry.

As I am writing this book, the ministry is just coming out of reorganized bankruptcy; the incredible property known as the Crystal Cathedral has been sold; and the future direction of the ministry, though now gaining a new strength and excitement, will be very different than that of its past.

These changes have caused tremendous suffering for my grandparents. But, in the end, they can find solace in the knowledge that they have changed millions of lives. Their ministry has even saved people from certain death! There are letters upon letters from people who stepped away from ledges, pulled guns away from their heads, got back up after falling to start their own business, or got an education. My grandparents inspired millions of people to live better lives and brought even more people to know God's love.

Churches come and churches go, but the impact they made can never be undone. My grandparents can find comfort in this knowledge. This is true for you as well. Your calling may not be as dramatic as theirs, but it doesn't mean it's less important. If you are breathing, you are making history. Don't despair. The good things you do today will stay good forever!

Heroic Happiness

If acting happy around others is a form of altruism, then acting happy around others, even while you suffer, is heroic. In order to be happy while we suffer, we must find meaning in our suffering. If our suffering comes from terrible or unending pain, we must find meaning through our heroic work and our sense of humor. If we suffer from guilt, we must walk the happy road of receiving forgiveness from God, confess our mistakes, and then walk the difficult but exciting road of reform. If we're suffering from change, we must remember that all our life's most treasured moments stay fixed and continue to affect the world in which we currently live.

No matter the form of suffering, we must find its

meaning. God can reveal to us the purpose of all suffering. He can heal us and give us strength, no matter how awful the trial. If you cannot find the meaning of your suffering, despair is at hand. For the sake of those around you, it is imperative to seek the meaning of your trial, to know what life is demanding of you, and to rise to the occasion. Only then can you live each day as a happy student of Christ even though you're suffering. If you do, you will set an incredible example of heroic happiness to all who know and love you.

CHAPTER FOUR

Gratitude and the Good Life

"Not having expectations does ensure
two beautiful things: minimum suffering over
unfulfilled goals and profound gratitude over goals
that are fulfilled. There is little in life that gives so
much at so little cost as not having expectations."
—Dennis Prager

Gratitude = Happiness

The Bible is a huge and wonderful book—a library, in fact—containing many books, all inspired by God. The book functions as the greatest source of textual authority for Christians around the world. One of the most common commandments in the Bible is the exhortation to be grateful to God. In fact, to the best of my knowledge, every book in the Bible mentions something about gratitude or thanks.

Though everyone seems to think gratitude is a good thing, few people see it as a moral imperative, and even fewer understand what a gift it is. Being a grateful person is a heavenly treasure, because gratitude, perhaps more than anything, is indelibly linked to happiness.

Not only does God command his people to be grateful, to have events or festivals that remind them to be thankful, but he wants them to be thankful because a thankful life is a happy life. Think about it. It is nearly impossible to picture a terribly unhappy person who is also thankful and grateful. Can you think of anyone who is wonderfully thankful and lives out of an inner sense of gratitude but still is unhappy? Happiness and gratitude are so linked that they are nearly the same thing. In order to be happy, we must be grateful! We must also rid our lives of the attitudes and patterns that cause us to be unthankful: comparing ourselves to others, a sense of entitlement, and clinging to our expectations.

A famous Bible story that deals with gratefulness is the story of the ten lepers. This is a magnificent story with a great deal to teach us about thankfulness and expectations. In the story, there are ten lepers; nine are Jewish and one is Samaritan. In Jesus's day, people were terrified of leprosy. Communities cast out lepers, pulling them from both family and synagogue, and viewed them as dirty and even cursed by God. Lepers rarely recovered. They had little hope of being with their loved ones again. Contracting leprosy was horrific on numerous levels.

The only thing worse than being a leper was being a Samaritan. This comes as a surprise to most, because "good Samaritan" is an endearing term in our culture. In Jesus's day, it certainly was not. The Samaritans were viewed as cursed half-breeds by the Israelites (because they were only part Jewish) and it was highly recommended that decent people not touch, look at, or associate with them. Jewish culture had bitter contempt for Samaritans. Many people probably assumed that Jesus, who was a famous Jewish rabbi and healer, shared this acrimonious dislike of Samaritans.

When these ten lepers saw Jesus, they cried out for healing and help. Jesus, instead of healing the lepers on the spot, told them to present themselves to the Jewish priest, according to custom. They did this and were healed, but only the Samaritan returned to thank Jesus. Jesus, upon seeing only one leper return, became upset and asked after the other nine. The story ends there.

The most important question to ask is: why did the one Samaritan return but not the nine Jewish lepers? The answer: the Samaritan didn't think he would be healed. He had no expectations but went to the priest with hope, not entitlement. Can you imagine the ten of them on their way to show themselves to the priest? They must have felt pretty optimistic about their situations—why would Jesus send them if they weren't going to be healed?

The only one who'd had any doubt was the Samaritan. He most likely thought that Jesus had assumed he was Jewish as well. He must have thought, *Imagine me, a Samaritan, showing myself to a Jewish priest!* He most likely believed Jesus spoke to him only by mistake. When his body was restored, he was surprised and more thankful than the rest. There is no doubt the others were thankful, but they weren't as thankful and, therefore, as happy as the Samaritan. Why? Because the Samaritan took a step of faith, but he did it without expectation or entitlement. He went with only a small glimmer of hope.

The first thing we must learn from this story is that expectations diminish gratitude and, therefore, happiness. I want to clarify here that expectations and faith are very different. The Samaritan never doubted Jesus's power to heal; he only doubted his entitlement to receive such healing.

Expectations Are the Enemy

Expectations diminish happiness, because they diminish gratitude. In business school and throughout my life, I've listened to many motivational speeches, and I've often heard speakers express the importance of having great expectations. "When you apply for a job, you ought to expect to get it," people would say. Many professionals love to give the advice that one should have big expectations, which lead to bigger goals and more confidence. This is a mistake, because big goals and big assumptions are not the same thing. You can play the lottery. Winning the lottery is a big goal, but you certainly don't *expect* to win. Big goals are great, but expectations are not, because they decrease the surprise factor.

If you expect to get something, say a job, a Christmas gift, or a particular inheritance, and you do in fact get it, you are far less surprised and thankful, because you simply got what you assumed was coming to you. It doesn't mean you will be unthankful. It simply means you will be less thankful than if you hadn't expected it. Also, the reverse is true. Imagine you receive an unexpected inheritance you didn't know was coming from a great-aunt who loved you dearly. How surprised you would be! What gratitude and joy you would feel!

Dennis Prager has written some wonderful things about expectations and gratitude. He uses the example of actors in Hollywood. Tens of thousands of people come to Los Angeles from all over the world to make it big in the city of glitz and glamour. They dream of stardom. Many times, famous actors claim that they "always knew" they would "make it big."

But you never hear the story of all the servers at

the restaurants and bars in LA who also "always knew" and didn't get anywhere. There are so many actors and musicians who are unhappy, because they had vast expectations of fame and wealth...and got nowhere. Some fall into deep depression or turn to substance abuse. Does this mean they shouldn't attempt to become actors? No, of course not. But, their unrealistic assumptions easily create a disillusioned life of animosity, although I'm not so sure those who do achieve celebrity status are all that happy, either.

Prager says, the greater number of expectations you have in your life, the less happy you will be, because the less grateful you will be. Everyone has expectations in life; however, we should know what they are and understand whether or not they are realistic.

According to Prager, there are definite, realistic, and unrealistic expectations. Definite expectations include the immutable laws of physics. For example, I know when I go to sip my hot coffee that gravity will keep it in my cup. I know the sun will rise in the morning and set in the evening. These are obvious and don't really play a role in the topic at hand. However, the other two—realistic and unrealistic expectations—do.

Unrealistic Expectations

We all have unrealistic expectations in life. The

problem is that we don't always recognize they are unrealistic or unfair, and we allow them to poison our life. Unrealistic expectations can include the expectation of achieving Hollywood stardom, but there are also day-to-day examples. It's unrealistic to expect to get a job for which you have applied for, for instance.

Imagine that a young man applies for a job, feels the interview went fabulously, and believes with all his heart that he got the job. Maybe the interview hinted at it. Maybe the interviewer smiled a lot and said, "We're definitely going to call you." In the end, he takes out his friends and celebrates prematurely, only to find that he didn't get the job. He will be unhappy. Even if he does get the job, he is likely to have that "of course, I got the job" attitude. He won't be as thankful or surprised as if he had not been expecting to get it.

We also put unrealistic assumptions on our spouses and children. If you always expect your husband to bring you flowers or your wife to always want intimacy, you have unrealistic expectations. If you assume your spouse will always take out the trash, do the dishes, or cook for you, you have unrealistic expectations, and you will be less grateful when you do receive these kindnesses.

Nobody wants his or her spouse to have unrealistic assumptions in marriage. Many times, spouses inadvertently encourage their husbands or wives not to do good things. If they do good things too many times, it becomes a new expectation! *I don't want to do the*

69

dishes three nights in a row, or it will become my new job, they might think.

We unfairly expect our children to thrive and succeed in all the things in which we didn't thrive and succeed. We have unrealistic assumptions about sports, tastes, and grades. This creates terrible unhappiness for both the children and the parents. Encourage your family. Desire things for your family. Believe in your family. But never impose unfair expectations on them.

If you look hard enough, you are likely to find many unrealistic expectations in many facets of your life. They exist at work, at home, at restaurants, in friendship, and in church. They harm you and others while sapping happiness and gratitude. Unfair and unrealistic assumptions are your enemies. Get rid of them, and become a better person.

Realistic Expectations

Of course, there are some perfectly realistic expectations in life. We live with them every day, and it's fully understandable that you have them. However, it's a good thing to also diminish even your realistic expectations. Prager's favorite example is that of waking up healthy. He says it is perfectly realistic to expect to wake up healthy every morning, but it is not definite. He says that we ought to give up even this type of expectation, because someday we won't wake up healthy. It is a sure thing that the sun will rise tomorrow, but it is not a sure thing that you will wake up healthy.[ix]

Although we don't want to live in fear, what if we gave up the expectation of going to bed healthy? That way, every day we are healthy is a good day! It is realistic to expect to be healthy, but we've abandoned that expectation, too. For every day we go to bed healthy, we can take a deep breath and thank God for a wonderful and healthy day. Some people can't say that tonight. What if God's people were like that? What if we were thankful every day because we're still alive?

It's also perfectly realistic to assume your husband or wife will keep his or her marriage vows and be faithful till death parts you. However, wouldn't marriages be better if we could abandon even this very realistic expectation? I don't mean trading it for fear. That would cause more harm than good. I simply mean never giving up the chase. As a pastor, I have talked with too many people who found themselves alone in bed one morning after thirty years of marriage. Their spouse just left. It always hits like a load of bricks.

If every day you woke up and thanked God that you had your wife or husband, how much fuller would your life and marriage be? If every day you woke up grateful that someone had sacrificed and given so much to be with you, how much happier would your marriage be? It's better to diminish our expectations and reduce what we expect of people. It makes us more grateful in the end.

Reducing expectations does not mean reducing desire. Expectations lead to entitlement. Entitlement leads to anger and bitterness. Desire is a fine thing, if you desire the right things. Desire can help you set goals, work hard, accomplish some of those goals, and feel rewarded for a job well done.

But beware of desire married to expectation. When expectation is attached to your desire, you probably feel entitled. In the end, when you achieve your desired goal, you'll be less likely to enjoy the reward. You may desire a girl's phone number and ask her for it, but beware the guy who feels entitled to it. You may desire your kids to do well at music and sports, but woe to the parents who expect their kids to excel at those things. You may long to sing well or learn an instrument, desire to make money, and crave travel. You may even take measures to do those things, but if you feel entitled to them, they will bring you little pleasure. You may long for a wonderful marriage and good friendships, but don't expect them. Expectation ruins the thankful heart.

Reducing your expectations does not mean reducing your faith in God. In fact, many confuse faith in God with expectation and feelings of entitlement. This unbiblical and nonsensical worldview has led to great harm in the church. It is mature and good to trust in God during hardship, to ask him to pull you through, and to illuminate your life with meaning in the midst of tragedy.

It is childish, however, to treat God like a vending machine. Too often, people expect God to do things just the way they want. They want him to meet their needs on their terms. They don't think to change their way of living, their choices, or their will. They just want God to give them something. This is not Christian maturity. Faith is trusting God that he wants the best for you.

I don't give everything to my three-year-old daughter just because she wants it. I know better than she does. Neither does our heavenly Father, who knows best, always give us everything we want. Have faith that he treasures you more than you could possibly understand. Know that you are in his care, even when things don't go your way. This is true faith.

Abandoning Outcomes

Faith in God is not the same as laying assumptions or entitlements upon God. Faith in God is abandoning our expectations by totally trusting, loving, and obeying a God who treasures us. One of the best ways we can live in God's presence and life is to, in the words of Dallas Willard, abandon outcomes.

The principle of abandoning outcomes means that we live each day without expecting any particular outcome from God. We simply live in the present. This principle is a difficult one to follow. It's so easy for me to find my identity in what I have, what I do, or what people say about me. But this is not how God views me. He views me as his beloved son who doesn't have to do anything to earn his love. It's a gift given to me at birth, and it will never leave me. When I forget this gift of God's love, I am driven to force things to happen my way, with or without God. This is not his way. In the end God wants us to be happy, living in his kingdom, whether things turn out just the way we want them to or not.

Abandoning outcomes is total submission to God, to the life he is preparing for you. It's an admission that you need him. We are all blind and hungry. He is our guide and our nourishment. Living in the kingdom of God now means I don't have to worry about what happens. God has it all figured out. I will strive, work hard, make goals, hope, and desire, but, no matter what happens, all outcomes are God's, not mine. He is the master. I don't have to worry, or expect, or feel entitled. I can just be thankful and, therefore, happy.

Gratitude Is the Heartbeat of Happiness

Gratitude and happiness are inseparable. The more thankful you are, the happier you are. I have come to believe this as a mathematical formula. The more things you are grateful for, the happier you are. People who are grateful receive more gifts. Thankful people are more likely to receive help with all kinds of things, like moving or finding babysitters.

Grateful people are a pleasure to be around, because they bless everyone around them with thankfulness. Their very spirits exude blessings. They can be a lighted lamp in a dark room. They constantly lift people up by reminding them of all life's blessings. Isn't thankfulness a choice? If gratitude and thankfulness are choices and are indelibly linked to happiness, then isn't our happiness a choice, in part?

A thankful spirit is at the core of happy living. This is why those before us have left so many traditions, both religious and cultural, to constantly bring us into a pattern of thankfulness. If you were raised in a Christian home, for example, it is likely you prayed before every meal—giving thanks for it. Sometimes we pray, "Bless this food to our bodies," but the best kind of prayer is, "Thank you, God, for this meal!" This prayer recognizes that everything good comes from God and that the one praying is blessed. It recognizes there might be others who don't have food. It recognizes that tomorrow, "that person could be me."

We celebrate events like Thanksgiving and share with one another what we are most thankful for. Every New Year's Eve, my dad used to take the whole family up to an old cabin at Big Bear Lake in the mountains. It was like something out of a book. There we were, with s'mores and hot chocolate, deep in conversation. We would always end the year saying what we were most thankful for. It was a memorable time that brought incredible warmth and happiness to a cold night. We would laugh and remember amazing stories or testimonies we would have forgotten otherwise. What a great way to end those years—with gratitude! God wants us to be thankful, because gratitude is the heartbeat of happiness.

The Science of Grateful Happiness

It's not just tradition and faith that teach us to be a thankful people. Science supports the idea as well. Robert Emmons, a professor of psychology at UC Davis, published a fascinating study in the *Journal of Personality and Social Psychology.*[x] In this study, doctors wanted to figure out from a scientific perspective what makes people happy. The study presents some stellar discoveries that reveal a great deal about happiness and human nature.

Emmons believed, based on his study, that all people have a "set point" of happiness. It appeared that, no matter what, people would always return to some middle point of happiness in their lives, regardless of what happened. For example, if an individual wins the lottery, his measured happiness will skyrocket for a period of about three months, but eventually he will return to the original measurement of happiness he had before—to the set point. Or, let's say the same person has a terrible car accident and loses the ability to walk. Now, the measured happiness will plummet for a period of time, but, after a short while, it will go back up to the original set point of happiness.

This was a profound discovery. It meant that circumstance had very little to do with an individual's long-term happiness. It debunked the popular myth that circumstance and happiness are related. Though the doctors tried many experiments to change the measurable long-term happiness of their subjects, only one thing was able to bring lasting sustainable happiness. There was only one thing that could permanently move the measured set point of happiness: the regular practice of daily thanks.

This amazing study involved 1,035 individuals in the test group, and 1,035 in the control group. The doctors gave the test group a simple assignment. They asked them to write a small list of five things they were thankful for once a week for a period of ten weeks. Each week, they had to write something new. Many (probably the unhappy ones) thought they would have a terrible time doing this, but in the end they were all able to manage some humble lists of thanksgiving.

Here's an example of an actual list:

1. I don't have a headache today.
2. I had a good lunch.
3. I have my family.
4. My socks keep my feet warm.
5. I made a joke and people laughed.

It appears that this person seemed to struggle to find five things to be thankful for, but all the test subjects were able to complete the task with some amazing results.

After ten weeks of practicing thankful reflection, the average measured set point of happiness per subject went up 25 percent. All subjects were more optimistic about life and their futures. Even more interesting, they were all healthier than they had been only ten weeks before. Many continued this practice after the experiment ended, and their continued growth in happiness didn't slow down. Their measured happiness continued to increase with each passing week—up to six months after the original test ended.

Emmons and his crew had found something wonderful. They were able to prove, at some subjective level, that happiness and gratitude are certainly linked. They climbed on board with what philosophy and religion have been saying for thousands of years. A grateful person is a happier person.

Another study by Chris Peterson, a psychology professor at the University of Michigan, revealed the same thing. He would often ask his students to write a "gratitude letter" to someone they "never properly thanked" and read it aloud to that person. He always heard great stories from his students about these "gratitude visits," but, ironically, he never wrote a "gratitude letter" himself, because he thought his own assignment was too "hokey."

Eventually, he decided to write a "gratitude letter," but he struggled to be serious and not cloud his thanks with jokes. Finally, he managed to write his letter and read it aloud to the person he had never thanked. He did it "straight from the heart." In the end, the act gave him such a euphoric joy that he decided to conduct a clinical study.

He saw that, in nearly every instance, those who wrote heartfelt letters of thanks and read them aloud to the people for whom they were intended experienced about a month of increased happiness and joy. Although we want to be careful about not defining happiness as just a feeling, there is clearly a connection between thankful living and happiness: the flourishing of the human soul.

Gratitude Brings Us Closer to God

There is something deeply spiritual going on when an individual chooses to practice thankfulness. Being thankful for the simple blessings in life reorients your view of the world. You begin to feel not so alone, because something or someone is blessing you. When you no longer feel alone, the "God-shaped hole" in your soul begins to fill with the light and goodness of our creator.

When an individual writes a gratitude list, who are they thanking? In the example given previously about the person who lists socks as an item to be thankful for, who is this person thanking? Do we suppose he is thanking the factory worker who helped the machines knit his socks together? Maybe he's thankful for the Fruit of the Loom Corporation for their great business practices and their ability to get socks to him in such a swift and inexpensive way. Doubtful. Thankfulness is euphoric and uplifting, because when a person quietly and secretly writes that he is thankful for socks, he is thankful to God. Though he or she may not say this or believe it outright, there is something in his or her soul that looks up to the heavens with thanks. Thankfulness lifts the human spirit, because it is a subconscious choice to believe "God is blessing me." God responds to the choice with affection and love. He blesses the grateful heart with true happiness: "I will praise God's name in song and glorify him with thanksgiving" (Psalm 69:30, NIV).

Be the Thankful Samaritan

In the end, it may be that everyone around you is unthankful and bitter about life. You cannot, for the sake of your own soul, be like these people. You must transcend and control your emotions, choosing to be thankful instead of negative. The Samaritan leper returned when the other nine did not. He was more blessed than the others, because he was thankful. He did not feel entitled to or expect his healing. He abandoned all outcomes. It was Jesus's choice, not his.

Trusting Christ with all outcomes and abandoning expectations freed the Samaritan to be unlike everyone else: a happy, flourishing, and life-filled disciple of Christ.

Living every day from a centered place of thankfulness allows life to blossom into a deep and pervasive sense of well-being. Thankfulness changes the way we view the world and blesses everyone around us. Becoming a thankful person is becoming a happier person.

CHAPTER FIVE

Real Pleasure

"There was some one thing that was too great
for God to show us when he walked upon our
earth; and I have sometimes fancied that
it was his mirth."
—G.K. Chesterton

The God Who Laughs

Does God really feel pleasure? Mirth is a burst of joy and laughter. Can God express this kind of emotion? Does he ever smile or chuckle at a funny joke? Would God ever do something like tell a joke? Many of us imagine God as a stoic who is either angry or cold. Many of us grew up with the image of God as a judge and nothing else. We appeal to his mercy, as we should, but it feels crazy to appeal to his sense of humor. How could God have such a thing?

It has come to my attention that God not only laughs but is the most joy-filled, inspired, and interesting being in the universe. He is everywhere and has created everything that is good in the world. He takes incredible joy in his creation and says over it, "It is good." God smiles and God laughs, because God invented smiles and laughter. It's easy to think of tears being holy and silence being reverent, but what about a party? Can God be part of a party?

On several occasions, the Bible refers to God as "the God who laughs." Proverbs 17 says, "A merry heart is a great medicine!" God established for the Jewish people all sorts of festivals where they were commanded to spend sometimes up to a week eating, drinking, laughing, and celebrating. It's a part of his commandment to them to have fun, laugh, and celebrate in remembrance of the God they serve. Because of problems like substance abuse, reckless behavior, or debauchery, many Christians and religious people don't have a warm view of parties, celebration, or laughter, but God commanded them.

This chapter discusses how to live in God's kingdom with wonder, mirth, laughter, and, especially, pleasure. Although pleasure is not happiness, God wants us to have the right kind of good pleasure that comes from celebration and a pervasive sense of well-being. We can derive pleasure from all sorts of things, but not all kinds of pleasure are good for us.

Too often, we throw out pleasure altogether, when we ought to do a better job of recognizing what types of pleasure bless our lives and what types of pleasure harm them. Sometimes we can overdo a pleasurable thing that's normally good for us. Eating a fresh-baked, warm cinnamon roll imparts a good kind of pleasure, but not if we eat eight rolls in one sitting. I have actually done that, because I love cinnamon rolls.

Of the festivals in ancient Israel, four were pilgrim festivals. These were wonderful celebrations. Jews from all over the Near East would travel hundreds of miles to worship at the temple in Jerusalem. These were times of great religious celebration, as well as not-so-religious celebration. Because so many people came to the great city, bringing their money with them, there were all sorts of both wonderful and awful things available to the tourists attending the festival. There was great food, dancing, worship, and storytelling, but there was also prostitution, the opportunity to over-indulge, and mind-altering substances.

In those days, the pilgrims sang psalms, written specifically for the pilgrimage, on their way to Jerusalem (Psalms 120–134). If you had lived in those times, you might have seen a Jewish family walking on the King's Road, heading south, singing some happy song. If you had stopped them with a salutation and asked them what they were up to, they would have told you, with smiles on their faces, that they were going to Jerusalem for the great celebration. Then they would have continued singing happily.

Much like Christmas hymns, these psalms were meant to keep the pilgrims focused on what was truly important when going to a place with so many temptations. Pilgrims sang these songs to honor God and his story with his people. Pilgrims sung these psalms to prepare their hearts for an experience both pleasurable and deeply religious. The songs were meant to center them on God. My favorite pilgrim psalm is 131, which talks specifically about finding pleasure from God before experiencing the pleasures of the world.

> Jehovah my heart has no lofty ambitions
> My eyes do not look too high
> I am not concerned with great affairs
> Or marvels beyond my scope
> Enough for me to keep my soul tranquil and quiet
> Like a child in its mother's arms
> As content as a child that has been weaned
> Israel, rely on Jehovah, now and always.
> —Psalm 131

People sang this beautiful song with joy and mirth, perhaps in a round with all sorts of harmonies. The pilgrims, knowing where they were going and the temptations they might encounter there, would remind themselves that the greatest pleasure comes from depending on God. They asked to be tranquil and quiet in the presence of God's holy hill. They did not ask for bright lights, loud music, and extreme experiences.

As I write this book, this song hits home for me, because we just had a baby. My son Cohen was just born and is breast-feeding from his mother. He is just a little baby, but he depends, with every ounce of his little baby being, on his mother. She is his source of food and comfort. It's amazing how upset he gets when he is hungry. He is sleeping peacefully in his little crib and little pajamas when, all of a sudden, he begins to shriek! It's like he's experiencing some pain. You'd think the house was on fire or someone had just been murdered. Within seconds, tears are rolling down his chubby cheeks, his arms and legs are flailing, and his jaw shakes with every wail.

Instantly, his mother picks him up and begins feeding him. He makes noises while he drinks that sound like he hasn't had milk in ages. Everything is so dramatic. The best time is when he finishes. With a full stomach, he pulls away from his mother with the biggest, happiest, baby smile you have ever seen. His eyes are closed, his mouth is in a chubby open smile from ear to ear. Then he stretches and falls gently to sleep.

This is the very humble and sweet image the Jewish people used to sing about: the great pleasure they can derive only from God. They look to God as the one who brings nourishment to their souls. He is the only one who can put a real smile on their faces. They are not interested in all those other worldly experiences in Jerusalem. In God's presence, they are like babes in their mothers' arms. He fills their spiritual stomachs and brings rest to their tired souls. He is worth every mile of travel, every expense, and every danger, because of the great sustaining pleasure he brings.

What a wonderful way to sing about God. Will these people derive pleasure from the wine, the dancing, the storytelling, and the singing they encounter? Absolutely! But their first and best pleasure, their only reason for celebrating, is God, the God who laughs. If you can't find pleasure in him, you won't find real, lasting pleasure in anything else.

The Numbness

Many of God's gifts bring us healthy pleasure, but there are so many more things that bring unhealthy pleasure. In our new technological age, we have access to a limitless number of pleasurable things, most of which are not altogether bad. However, we have these things in such great abundance that we recklessly consume them without limit or restraint. When this happens, we easily form addictions to stimulation, entertainment, and fun—to the point that we become numb. In our great quest for pleasure, these pleasurable things lose their potency, and we are caught in a trap of our own making.

At the turn of the twentieth century, apocalyptic

literature had become quite popular. The industrial revolution was in full swing, and everything in the Western world was changing. Airplanes, cars, radio, and electricity were coming at people whether they were ready or not. Many believed that this was the end of an age, that Christ would return, or that we would undo ourselves. Authors George Orwell and Aldous Huxley wrote famously on this subject. Orwell's famous novel *1984* envisages a world where a police power has completely taken over, and everyone is dependent on the government. In this brutal world, mankind has lost all freedom, and people live as slaves to an oppressive power.

The other, less famous author, Huxley, didn't see the end of the world in this way at all. He believed the end of the world would come because of overstimulation and drug abuse. He believed that people would happily become slaves in exchange for pleasure and entertainment.

Neil Postman, the legendary American media theorist from New York University, was the first to compare these two authors. He believed, like Huxley, that television and the overindulgence of entertainment was dangerous and bad for society, more dangerous than a police power. He believed that every part of civil and religious life, as well as education and politics, was in grave danger because of the advent of television.

These great thinkers, who are now dead, had no clue that we would be in the place we are now. The average person is not only addicted to television, but to laptops, iPhones, iPads, MP3 players, and Facebook. We live in a world where, at every moment, we are terrified of boredom and distract ourselves with technology and social media.

Although all this has, by no means, led to the end of the world, it has led to feelings of serious unhappiness and emptiness. We have a million ways to connect with others. I can Skype, right this instant, with my friend in the Netherlands and my friend in China. At all times, I can see where my friends are and what they are doing on Facebook. People share pictures and videos constantly. I can text or call anyone, anywhere, at any time. Even now, I know my inbox has one hundred e-mails. Yet, with all these ways to connect, we are lonelier than ever. With all these forms of entertainment, we are more bored than ever.

What on earth is happening? Though all of these things, in essence, are not bad, they are so abundant that we submit all of our attention with total abandon. We don't realize that all technology comes with a price. That unknown cost slowly creeps up on us and eventually forces us to pay. There is a good chance that all the e-mails, phone calls, texts, and Facebook posts don't get you excited and might even make you cringe. This is because the bright lights, flashing LED screens, and loud noises are actually unhealthy.

It's a psychological condition called *anhedonia*. I first read about the term in Dr. Archibald Hart's book,

Thrilled to Death.[xi] Anhedonia is the medical term for a dysfunction of the brain that causes a patient to be unable to experience pleasure. It is a kind of numbness to the world. The anhedonic person has difficulty crying or laughing. This person can feel little or nothing from things that used to give great pleasure. It is not crippling like depression, though it can lead to that. It's a constant boredom. It used to be believed that anhedonia was an ailment limited only to those suffering from schizophrenia or depression. Now, anhedonia is commonplace and affects the happiness of millions of people. Have you ever felt this numbness or sense of constant boredom?

In 1954, two scientists, Olds and Milner, were conducting tests on rats in order to understand how the brain functions. One of the earliest tests they conducted involved attaching electrodes to different parts of a rat's brain to measure stimulus and response. The first result they got came from discovering the rage center of the rat's brain. Every time they fired off an electronic pulse, the rat would break into a terrible rage.

This was a startling find and very curious indeed. But the greater discovery came just after, when the scientists moved the electrodes, just slightly, and discovered the *locus accumbens*, the pleasure center of the brain. Scientists learned that every time they sent a pulse to this part of the rat's brain, the rats' brains released dopamine, causing the rats to experience a great deal of pleasure. Dopamine is the chemical in the brain that causes pleasure.

Soon, they set up more tests to better understand the rat's brain. The first test included a small pedal the rat could tap with its foot, triggering the electrode and the pleasure center of its brain. Every time the rat hit the pedal, its brain would release dopamine, causing the sensation of pleasure. Amazingly, the rat hit the pedal over and over again, sometimes thousands of hits within an hour. The rat would forego natural, instinctual needs like food and sex to keep receiving hits of dopamine. The scientists set up electrically charged grids between the rat and the pleasure pedal. Even though the grid was terribly painful, the rat would willingly walk across it to get another hit of dopamine. Many rats even chose to hit the pedal to the point of death.

Although these tests are troubling, and possibly unethical, they also revealed something about the human brain, illuminating the current predicament in which we find ourselves. The constant hit of dopamine in the pleasure center of the brain caused anhedonia in the rats. They were unable to get enough hits of the electrode, because with each hit, they received diminishing returns. The more the rats hit the pedal, the less pleasure they received, because they were addicted. They hit the pedal over and over again, but they could never be satisfied and only fell further into the depths of addiction.

Though scientists used an electrode to trigger the brain's pleasure center, they have discovered that many other stimuli can trigger the human brain's pleasure center as well, such as loud noises and bright lights. Scientists are beginning to understand the tremendous impact that technologies like television and computers have on the way our brain functions. Human beings trigger their pleasure center every time they watch TV or play video games. Every time they listen to loud music on the iPhone or in their car, they hit the pleasure pedal. Every time there are loud, bright explosions in the theater, they hit the pedal. Adrenaline, stress, and the constant consumption of electronic media release dopamine and cause pleasure, but they do so with diminishing returns. You will never have enough. As a result, many people are in a constant anhedonic state, which has become known as the "hedonic treadmill."

People have become addicted to technology and to the way it stimulates the brain. They continue to hit the pedal over and again, and, with each hit, they need louder, bigger, brighter, and more shocking stimuli. Like drug abuse, people are harming themselves with their addiction to overstimulation, and as a result, they are unable to feel pleasure in the simple things. With each hit, their pleasure threshold goes up, and their ability to feel pleasure goes down. There has been a tremendous amount of work on this topic, and we could continue to explore the topic. But, for our purposes here, simply understand that pleasure derived from technology is highly addictive and can cause serious neurological problems in the human brain.

The quick answer for how to undo the damage caused by technological overstimulation is simple. Use these things much less, get more sleep, and return to activities that bring healthy, long-lasting pleasure, such as like walks, prayer, conversations with friends, and reading good books. (For a great book on this topic, read *Thrilled to Death* by Archibald Hart).

Pleasure Is a Spice

Every kid loves candy. Halloween and Easter seem almost like the same holiday to children, because they get as much candy as they want. I remember one particular Halloween. I was not a little kid anymore, but a kid nonetheless, and I was given more freedom—the freedom to trick or treat with my friends, the freedom to fill an entire trash bag with sometimes ill-gotten candy, and the freedom to eat as much as I wanted.

Though I thought this was a great blessing, this freedom to do whatever I want was a curse for me. I went crazy. I woke up in my room in the middle of the night upon a blanket of candy wrappers, sicker than I'd ever been.

Pleasure is a peculiar thing. It's at its best when carefully moderated. Food is delicious, but if we eat too much, we get fat. Hobbies are great, but if we overdo them, we neglect the truly important things in our life.

Making love to your spouse can be amazing, but pornography, sexual addiction, and cheap sex will destroy the soul. Nearly all normative pleasures can be overdone: TV, the Internet, wine, and games. Why do we do this to ourselves? Why do human beings constantly take pleasurable things and turn them into addictive curses?

The seventeenth-century mathematician and philosopher, Blaise Pascal, said every person has a "God-shaped hole" in his or her soul. For some, the idea of God is too broad, overwhelming, or unbelievable, and he is not placed in this God-shaped chasm. Because of this, we continue to wander in an ongoing sense of loneliness, but we don't know why. We are busy but unproductive. We never have enough time and are always flooded with things to do. We live exhausting lives, but we can't stop, lest we feel unproductive or bored. We are living from an empty place, an empty hole.

Sometimes, when we stumble upon a sweet pleasure, perhaps it helps us relax or escape, we have the strange sensation this inner hole has been filled. It hasn't. We typically find this out far too late, after we've become addicted to whatever we've tried to force into this empty void.

This is the primary, most typical reason people become addicted to the normal pleasures of life. We try to shove food, shopping, money, women, friends, or beer down the hole, but, in the end, these simple and nice things can become a curse. They've become idols. God gave us these things to bless us, but if we don't live from a centered place in God's love, we unintentionally craft these things into idols. It has been happening for thousands of years, which is the precise reason the first of the Ten Commandments is "Thou shalt have no other gods before me."

If we make our relationship with God, and following Christ, the most important priority in our lives, we will be much less likely to abuse simple pleasures. Instead, these simple things—like a cool glass of wine at the end of the day, or a piece of rich chocolate cake after dinner—can bless our lives immensely. We see them as God's blessings rather than use them to make ourselves feel better temporarily or escape our lives. If that "God-shaped hole" is filled with God, and nothing else, we can now enjoy many of the pleasures of life in safety. Everything will be in its right place. Sex, candy, alcohol, TV—they can all bless our lives now, because we don't need them. We have the full understanding that God is the only thing we need. All those other things are his little pleasures.

As Prager tells us, pleasure is like a spice and must be used with "passionate moderation." Think of the many pleasures available to us as the many spices in the kitchen of life. A chef, one of the greatest in the world, is making his signature sauce. He is showing his apprentice how much of each spice is necessary to achieve the perfect flavor. As he adds just a pinch of this, or a dash of that, he whispers to himself, "careful...careful..." He knows that he needs just the right amount. He wouldn't ever consider making the sauce without these important and wonderful spices; it would be tasteless and boring. But he knows that he must not overdo it. He is using the spice in the sauce with "passionate moderation."

In life, simple daily pleasures are given to us to bring excitement and fun, but we must regard them with respect. They have the power to overcome us if we overdo them. Many of us find a spice we like and dump the whole bag into the sauce. We say, "Man, this is going to taste great!" In the end, we are repulsed, or worse. We get used to overly spicy sauce and say the really good stuff is "not salty enough."

The daily pleasures should be a blessing, and you shouldn't live without them, but they are the spice, not the food. Thank God for all the daily pleasures of life, but never try to make the daily pleasures into God himself. With wisdom, enjoy the blessings in life with a healthy, passionate moderation. Life will be more fun and interesting, and you won't get caught in a trap of your own making.

Godly Pleasures

It is easy to overdo TV, the Internet, alcohol, shopping, food, and many other simple pleasures of life, but there are some pleasures that can be far more pleasurable than these. The pleasures, mentioned above, have diminishing returns. The more you use them, the more you think you need them, while you simultaneously derive less pleasure from them.

There are other kinds of pleasures that become more enjoyable the more you enjoy them. These pleasures I will call godly pleasures. Godly pleasures can't become addictive, because they bring you closer to God, rather than replacing him. They cause you to pay attention to life, rather than help you escape from it into a fake reality. They bring you closer to people, because you aren't drawn to them out of your own neediness. You come to them because godly pleasures have made you a more secure and centered person. Though there are limitless examples of godly pleasures, let me tell you some of mine.

I love sitting under the avocado tree in my back-yard with a cup of coffee and a good book or the Bible. I love to get up early, before anyone else is awake, and walk around Peter's Canyon, a beautiful state park near my house. It has hundreds of acres of wildlife, with game trails, all kinds of birds and plants, and trees. On warm days, there is usually a cool breeze that gently comes in off the water in the natural reservoir. I pray there. I love to go to the mouth of Dana Point Harbor and watch the boats go in and out. I love playing chess with strangers. I love to water the plants in my yard with my three-year-old daughter. I love going on simple walks around the old town or farmers market with my wife. I love playing Chopin on the piano in my garage...

There are pleasures in life that, somehow, bring you closer to God and people, even though, in essence, they seem to have nothing to do with God or people. They do. These godly pleasures enrich the life of the person who discovers them. They grow in potency with each experience. Godly pleasures teach us to live life with childlike wonder and, from that place, to live with smiles and laughter, or rather, mirth.

There is a reason Jesus said the children will inherit the kingdom of God. They see the world in a different way than everybody else does. They see the world with fresh eyes. Things we may have seen a thousand times, that we don't even notice any more, are wondrous to children. This is why Dostoyevsky said, "The soul is healed by being with children."

Children remind us of what we too often forget. The world is magical and wondrous. They see it every day with awe and excitement; the bright colors of a butterfly, the beauty of a dandelion, a bird perched on a branch, or a Chihuahua sleeping against a chain-link fence. These things are interesting, exciting, and new. Children are not concerned with the news, politics, or reputation. Although we, as adults, must stand up for our responsibilities, our souls are easily harmed by forgetting that we live in the amazing world God crafted for us. Children remind us of this.

Once, I decided, in a moment of rest, that I would

try to see the world in the same way I had seen it when I was a boy. I was sitting on my porch at night, after everyone had gone to bed. It was a dark, but moonlit, warm, summer evening. In the top left corner of the porch overhang, a spider began to weave its web. Normally, my response would be to grab the broom and be rid of this pest, but I was watching as a boy now, you see. It was amazing.

This spider glided from one side to the other, crafting with perfection its little web. Across and across again it went, then in circles. It took forever. It was beautiful. A thought came to mind. Nobody ever taught this spider to make this little web. It just knows. It's not like when he was a little spider kid, he went off to web-making school where he got a degree in web engineering. His mother didn't take him out and show him step by step. It was instinct, the word we use instead of magic, because it sounds more scientific. Somehow, this spider knows how to make a perfect spider web.

I then tried to imagine a bunch of humans, with engineering degrees, trying to craft a larger web to scale. They could probably pull it off, but they would have a terrible time of it, especially if they had to do it the same way the spider did. Seeing the spider through the eyes of a child, rather than those of a concerned homeowner, allowed me to see God's purpose and design within the spider. In fact, in a roundabout way, it allowed me to see God's purpose and design within myself.

Though we are not called to be childish, we are called to be childlike. This means living in the world with a sense of wonder, never taking for granted the gifts of God's common grace to us.

My wife and I love traveling, when we get the chance. Whenever we go to a new place, we are filled with wonder and excitement. We listen to the languages and the music. We try all the different types of food slowly and savor them with admiration. We point at everything: this building, that painting, this famous monument, or that shop. Everything is interesting, because we're really looking. We've created space and prepared ourselves to take it all in. When we get home, we look at pictures, tell stories to our friends, and wonder when and where we will go next.

Once, I was walking around the town I live in, the place I'm completely used to, and I saw some travelers who were clearly from another country. They were looking around wide-eyed, pointing at everything and taking pictures. They were having trouble deciding, with joy, of course, whether or not they should go into this bakery to try the pastries or just get lunch at the wonderful restaurant across the street. Everything was marvelous to them. It struck me. They were doing in my boring town, the one I'm so used to, what I do when I go traveling.

I thought to myself, *What if I could be a traveler*

every day, no matter where I am? What if I could see my boring little town with new eyes, the way these travelers on vacation see it? What if I did my best to enjoy every smell, the food, the people, the language, the buildings, just like I would if I were traveling? What if I could be a traveler every day? I have done just that and, consequently, have fallen more and more in love with my little town.

One of the greatest pleasures in life is seeing the world, as it actually is: a place of wonder in God's eternal care. His pleasure and creativity is in it. Every day is a gift, meant to be enjoyed and savored. There is no reason that this new way of seeing and enjoying the world shouldn't cause us to smile, tell jokes, and laugh. Of course, there are some jokes we shouldn't tell, and there are some things we shouldn't laugh at, but laughing, smiling, and enjoying the company of others are great things. Smiles are divine, and laughter is holy. God is the God who laughs and cheerfully wants his children to be filled with his joy.

If we can find our very first and most important pleasure in God's life alone, then all the other good pleasures of this world can bless our lives immensely. We can enjoy a good meal with friends, a cup of coffee with a good book, crack up at a hilarious joke, and live life boldly, with a smile on our face. Somberness and seriousness are not typically good testimonies for what God has supposedly done in our life. If God is deep within our bones, we ought to be mirthful, filled with humor and celebration. This is a great testimony for what he's done. Enjoy the world in which God has carefully placed you. Enjoy the richness of life God's way, and don't be afraid to smile and even laugh along the way.

CHAPTER SIX

The Unquenchable Thirst

"There are two ways to become rich in this world:
get more or want less."
—Hawaiian Proverb

I was sitting at my favorite little pub. It's a wonderful place, very authentic looking, with old wood and little candles on the walls. There is always a fire going in the little brick fireplace, even though it's in sunny California. There are not many windows, but they're made of stained glass with fake lighting behind them, maybe to make it look more like typical English bad weather is looming outside. But the thing that made it the most authentic on this particular night was the drunken Scottish family sitting just across the way from me, talking just loudly enough that I could hear every other phrase they said.

The oldest one bellowed out what must have been a hilarious joke in a thick Scottish accent. He said, "Around us you have the English, the Irish, the Scottish, and the Welsh. You know how you know the difference?" To my despair, I couldn't seem to make out all the obviously funny things he said about each group, but I got the punch line: "...and the Irish don't know what they want and won't rest until they get it!" That made me smirk, especially since my heritage on my Mom's side is entirely Irish. You see, I've got a little bit of that myself—that nagging sense of always wanting something, even though I'm not sure what it is. Of course, I don't have that sense because of my four pints of Irish blood. I have that sense because I'm human.

Every human being has an insatiable appetite for something, even when he or she doesn't know what it is. Life is very often like the proverbial donkey with a carrot dangling in front of him, just out of reach. We put one foot in front of the other but perpetually fail to reach that juicy, orange carrot, even though it seems so close. Everyone, even the best of us, experiences this insatiability. If misunderstood, it can cause a great deal of confusion, frustration, and unhappiness.

Stay-at-home moms often give up careers, hobbies,

and fun to raise their kids, all while receiving sharp criticism from those who think they ought to work. Or, conversely, moms who need to work often miss their kids terribly and are treated badly for not staying home.

Men, even the very best of men, are often born with an insatiable sexual desire; they feel guilty. Artists fall into deep depression at times, because they are not able to create that one masterpiece, or sonata, or Pulitzer-caliber book. They destroy their wonderful creations and can never be satisfied with what they've made. The priest gives up any chance of marriage, or children, to dedicate his life to serving God. He wonders what it would have been like. The anorexic teenager looks in the mirror and sees a fat girl. She can never lose enough weight.

There is something deep in the heart of every individual that drives us, always, to want more, and more after that. It's impossible to satisfy us completely. Though we can never be totally satisfied, finished, and have enough, we can be happy.

Unfortunately, we allow the drive to attain more of this, or more of that, to ruin the treasures we already have. We are blinded by our love for money and safety. We often dream about winning the lottery or getting some incredible payout, so that we can finally start living life, a life of freedom. But that road never leads to happiness. It's a mirage. You are not lacking on the outside but within. We think we are poor, even though we may be rich with blessings not of this world. We are insatiable.

Jesus tells his students a story about a man with a huge grain harvest (Luke 12:13–21). This man has so much grain that there is not enough room to contain it all in his little silo. So, he builds a bigger one. After storing all his grain, he says, perhaps to the heavens, "Now that I have so much, I will eat, drink, and be merry." Then he dies. Jesus says this is what will happen to a man who is rich on earth but not rich in God's ways. Though very dark, this story is wonderful, because it shows that more grain, money, or a better job will not enrich your life unless you live under God's guidance and care.

We should assume that a great harvest would be a gift from God to this man, but his choices show his selfishness. He does not respond with meaningful choices, but selfish ones. Had the man lived, what would have been his life's purpose? With whom would he have eaten? To what toast would he have drunk? Perhaps he doesn't die as quickly as we presume. Maybe his life has so little meaning that, while living it up, he does nothing of value and dies.

You see, it doesn't matter if he dies instantly or twenty years after his great harvest. If he survives twenty years of meaningless and selfish living, he might as well have not lived at all. If only he had said, "What a blessing! All this grain! I will give some of it to those poor, suffering children in town." Or, "What a blessing!

Now I can devote my life to prayer, build a school, and help the widow next door pay the rent."

No, he didn't see his new wealth as God giving him the tools to make a difference. Rather, he believed the lie that he could bring satisfaction to all his desires. Before this great harvest, did he dream about living it up? Did he think about all the food, wine, and other pleasures he could attain? Did he think life was all about fulfilling selfish desires? Did he really think there was enough wine, women, or food in the whole world to fill his empty soul? He was blind.

It's amazing how many of our dreams revolve around satisfying our personal desires for pleasure, comfort, and freedom. We can spend hours looking at the kind of clothes we'll have, the kinds of places where we'll live, the types of women or men we'll be with, or the kinds of cars we'll drive. It's not that these things are bad. It's that they are, for the most part, meaningless. It's not even bad that we want them. It's that we think we'll have something more if we get them. We won't, because there will always be another car, house, romance, trip, and pair of shoes.

Again, it's not that we spend time thinking about these things, but how much time we spend doing that in comparison to what really matters. Instead, we should ask ourselves, "How can I be more like Christ?" or "How can I be a better spouse or parent?" or "How can I really impact my community or church?" or "Where is God at work, and how can I be a part of it?"

The shoes, cars, houses, and trips don't matter unless we use them for something meaningful. So, don't be fooled. You will never have enough unless you have enough right now. So, don't seek after these things, but seek after God's desires and goodness to enter a hurting, yet beautiful world. Then you will have enough.

Missing Tile Syndrome

No matter how spiritual we are, we will always struggle with the desires of this world. All of us are tricked, from time to time, into believing we are missing this or that, and that if we can only get it, we'll be happy. Sometimes, that can be true. If we get this or that, we might actually be a little happier, but I often doubt, even in those cases, that we'll be as happy as we expect to be. All of us have these things in our lives, these "if-only" desires that linger for so long.

Prager calls these missing, desired things in life "missing tiles," and he calls the obsessive desire to attain them "Missing Tile Syndrome."[xii] He paints the picture of a wonderful mosaic on the ceiling of, perhaps, a beautiful church or palace. This mosaic is beautiful and creates a wonderful picture, but as you look closely, you notice a tile from that mosaic is missing. For some reason, you cannot keep yourself from looking at it. You focus on it more and more until the bigger picture is almost unnoticeable. *Why don't they fix that?* you wonder. You look around hoping to find someone to explain to you why the curator would ruin such a beautiful work of art by allowing this little black dot to linger, distractedly, in its center. You begin to think, *This picture will only be beautiful if that tile can be filled.*

Prager says we view our lives like this beautiful mosaic. It's always missing something. He said he realized this when a bald friend of his told him that he was very self-conscious about his own lack of hair. He noted that everywhere he went, all he saw were men with hair. He couldn't help comparing their full heads of hair with his lack of hair, and this was causing him terrible unhappiness. Prager said he hadn't ever really even noticed his friend was bald in the first place, and yet his friend was allowing this missing tile to make every day an unhappy one.

This made me laugh, because my wife and I had a similar story. When we were trying to have a baby, it took us longer than we thought it should. We had been "trying" for eight or nine months with no luck. We thought we'd be pregnant right off the bat. Now, we were wondering if we could get pregnant at all. Hannah said that everywhere she went, she saw pregnant women, women with strollers, or mothers nursing their new infants. It was starting to bother her and bring her down as she began to have a huge missing tile in her life. We got pregnant soon after, and everything was fine, but it doesn't always work that way. Now that we have children, you can trust there are other missing tiles in our lives.

We compare. We think those who have what we want are happy, but they are comparing, too—maybe even comparing themselves to you. This is when the missing tiles become most distracting in our lives, when we allow ourselves to compare. Though many times it is possible to fill those empty tile spaces, we will never really have a perfect mosaic. In the end, life spent constantly and obsessively filling tiles will lead to unhappiness, if not madness. That's the way life works. You find the perfect tile, the right color and shape, you place it in its proper spot, and, just as it is glued and fixed firmly in its hole, another tile just ten feet to your right falls from the ceiling and shatters on impact. Enjoying the mosaic of life is not about putting every-thing in its rightful place but rather standing back and marveling at the masterpiece, black bits and all. If you can fill the hole, fine. But remember, even though more tiles will fall from their places, the picture will remain.

Don't compare your life to others. You don't really know what others have and what others don't have. Every parent on earth has told a child, "life is not fair," but I might amend that. Life is fairer than you think. We can't know everything about the ins and outs of others' lives, after all. You want what others have, and they want what you have. This is why envy is such a lie: "If you get what she has, you'll be happy." That's why envy is one of the big sins, one that breaks the Ten

Commandments. You easily hurt not only the person you envy but yourself, because you allow yourself to forget what you have and be haunted by the missing tile you think someone else has. If someone has what you do not, rejoice for them and give thanks to God. Step back and see what you have, and thank God all the more.

5 Percent Empty

All of us have more than we care to admit, especially here in the industrialized West. It's not lack, but our perceived lack, that gets us down most of the time. This is why I can't help but chuckle at the all-too-common cliché of the half-full or half-empty glass. In truth, most of our glasses are filled almost to the brim, as a glass ought to be filled. After all, if you are given a glass of water at a restaurant, they are not likely to fill it just to the very top, or it might spill. You fill it up about 95 percent. For those of us not in the midst of terrible tragedy or abject poverty, our glass is full to about where it should be—95 percent.

As humans, we ask why our glass is 5 percent empty and ask for just a little bit more. If you have three square meals a day, are not living in the midst of war, and are not ruled by an evil dictator, you've got a good percentage of the world beat. If you have a car, you're even further along. God is blessing you! But, for most of us, we see that missing 5 percent: the unattained job, the girl that doesn't want us, the inability to get six-pack abs, or the absence of the right kind of syrup at the grocery store. Rejoice. Your glass is so full that it would spill if you tried to carry it while running.

Freedom Is the Currency of Love

You're in a rest home for seniors. You've been visiting this rest home for a couple of years—visiting an old man named Joe, a man nobody likes because of his stern and unkind nature. You feel bad for Joe, so you make sure he has a friend as he lives out the twilight days of his life. Joe is on his deathbed, and, with his last words, he gives you the coordinates to a site where he has buried $30 million in gold bullion. He wants you, his only friend on earth, to have this fortune. Joe dies. You go after your new treasure.

Why? Why do you want the treasure? You dream about winning the lottery, perhaps. Why? Why would you want to have so much money that you wouldn't know what to do with it? Most people dream of treasure and vast sums of money because of the freedom they will bring. Freedom. This is the reason people want money. No more work. No more worry. No more risk. *I can go anywhere or do anything I want.* But will money really bring you freedom, and if freedom is what comes, is it something you really want? Has freedom been good for you in the past? Has this freedom, or perhaps we should say this lack of responsibility, made your life more meaningful, passionate, or interesting?

The book of Galatians teaches us about freedom. The young Saint Paul is writing to a church in Galatia filled with the Spirit of God. They are bearing his fruit of love, joy, and peace. There are some in the community who are trying to force a new legalism, outside the spirit of God's law, onto this church. Paul tells them to be free and live by the Spirit. However, toward the end of this book, he tells them not to use this freedom to "gratify the sinful nature, but rather serve one another in love" (Galatians 5:13). He is telling them the freedom given to them is not a freedom to do whatever they want, whenever they want, or to be immoral. Rather, when God gives us freedom, it is to serve our neighbor in love, to make the place we live a little brighter. For most of us, we don't see freedom as the new, exciting ability to pursue a better world. We see it as the new, exciting ability to be self-indulgent.

If you see freedom as the thing that will allow you to spend more time with your kids or your spouse, volunteer more, pray more, or spend more time creating something beautiful, congratulations! You are on the right track. For most of us, though, we don't really know what we would do with our freedom.

One way to know is to reflect on the past. Think about the last time you had a couple of days off work, or perhaps you had a summer vacation from the university. What did you do with that time? Did you spend more time in reflection? Did you start writing or painting or working on your piano sonata? Did you volunteer at a homeless shelter or take your wife on a much-needed date? How much time did you spend watching TV and staring at your computer screen? Do your eyes still hurt from the glare?

How you spend your free time is a good indicator of what you would actually do if you had more freedom. Would you be a better or worse person if you acquired a limitless amount of money and, therefore, freedom? We lament the freedom we don't have, but we don't really know what we would do if we actually had it.

There's little reason to lament, because there is a good chance much of the freedom you have lost, you have only lost because you willingly gave it away. If you want your freedom back, give back whatever it was you gave up your freedom to attain. Not so easy, is it? We cannot simply trade back, because, though we would get our freedom, we would lose a lot more in the process.

Freedom is the currency of love. The more love you have in your life, the less freedom you have. If you want to have meaningful relationships of any kind, it will cost you your freedom in increments. For every friend, every romance, every family member, you will spend some amount of freedom. Freedom will always be the cost.

When I first went to college, I had so much freedom that I didn't know what to do with myself. I had so much freedom and time, because I had so few relationships and so little responsibility. Soon, I started making friends. The more friends I had, the less freedom I had to study, sleep, or watch TV. As those friendships grew and matured, they required more of me.

Eventually, one of those friends became a girlfriend. There went more of my freedom, not just time. I could no longer date other people. Nor could I always go out with my other friends if I had plans with my new girlfriend. We got married, and more freedom was gone. We had kids, and ten times more freedom was gone. The freedom to sleep when I wanted, to go out with my wife when I wanted, and to spend money on what I wanted all disappeared after we had children. Would I trade any of that freedom? Not in a million years. This is because any meaningful relationship in one's life requires sacrifices of time, money, choice, sleep, and a whole slew of treasured things. Freedom is the cost, the currency spent on love. Surely other things can take away your freedom, too: jail, work, sickness, and the like. But with the freedom that remains, you can purchase love.

Every decision is a thousand renunciations. You can't have all freedom and all love. You need to understand this as you make the important relational choices in life. It's always important to ask, "Can I live without this degree of freedom to pursue this new aspect of love in my life?" The answer may be no. God may need you to keep a degree of your freedom to go after what he has called you to do.

Paul, for example, believed that it was better for some not to marry, so they could commit their lives to serving God. Roman Catholic priests still make this important choice today. I have a good friend who has remained a bachelor his whole life in order to better focus on business, philanthropy, and ministry. He knows he wouldn't be a good husband or father because he could not offer his freedom.

Many of us have children. That is one purchase you cannot return. It's easy to lament the loss of freedom because of what you've invested in your children, but never forget: raising good children is a ministry, too. Developing great children means developing a better generation of people. They need you. Though you have to put some things on hold because of your loss of freedom, you are doing something of infinite importance, not just for your kids, but for all the people who will live in the world. Your kids are someone else's parents, future spouses, coworkers, and patrons.

We cannot have all freedom and all love. We must continually choose and rest in the decisions we've made. We must know that if we want friends, marriage, and children, we won't have as much time to work on our hobbies or develop our careers. We must choose. This is life.

In the end, human beings are insatiable. We will always have missing tiles, unfinished symphonies, and we will even envy our neighbor from time to time, but we can still be happy. There will be places we won't visit, projects we won't finish, romances we won't have, children we won't bear, but we can be happy. We will spend our freedom on loving relationships, and we will be happy.

See the grand mosaic, not the little black hole. Enjoy the blessings of today, and don't throw away tomorrow. Rejoice in all that you've been given, and rejoice for those who have been given more. We will be dissatisfied, but we will be happy.

Endnotes

Chapter 1: The Fruit of Virtue

[i] Henri J. M. Nouwen, *Reaching Out: The Three Movements of the Spiritual Life* (New York: Doubleday, 1986), 24.

[ii] Tal Ben-Shahar, *Happier* (New York: McGraw-Hill, 2007), 8.

[iii] G.K. Chesterton, *Orthodoxy* (Peabody, Massachusetts: Hendrickson, 2006), 51-52

Chapter 2: Acting Happy Glorifies God

[iv] Dallas Willard, *The Divine Conspiracy: Rediscovering Our Hidden Life in God* (New York: HarperCollins, 1997), 62.

v   J.P. Moreland and Klaus Issler, *The Lost Virtue of Happiness: Discovering the Disciplines of the Good Life* (Colorado Springs: NavPress, 2006), 23.

Chapter 3: Happy While Suffering

vi   The Beatitudes read (Mathew 5: 3-10):

"Blessed are the poor in spirit,
for theirs is the kingdom of the heavens.

Blessed are those who mourn,
for they will be comforted.

Blessed are the meek,
for they will inherit the earth.

Blessed are those who hunger and thirst for righteousness,
for they will be filled.

Blessed are the merciful,
for they will be shown mercy.

Blessed are the pure in heart,
for they will see God.

Blessed are the peacemakers,
for they will be called sons of God.

Blessed are those who are persecuted for the sake of righteousness for theirs is the kingdom of the heavens."

vii Victor E. Frankl, *The Will to Meaning: Foundations and Applications of Logotherapy* (New York: Meridian, 1988). Also, for the full explanation of Frankl's life in the concentration camp, read his masterpiece, originally published anonymously, *Man's Search for Meaning.*

viii Dallas Willard, *The Divine Conspiracy: Rediscovering Our Hidden Life in God* (New York: HarperCollins, 1997).

Chapter 4: Gratitude and the Good Life

ix Dennis Prager, *Happiness Is a Serious Problem: A Human Nature Repair Manual* (New York: Harper, 1998), 55-64.

x Emmons, R.A. (1999). Religion in the Psychology of Personality. *Journal of Personality,* 67, 873-888.

Chapter 5: Real Pleasure

xi Archibald D. Hart, *Thrilled to Death: How the Endless Pursuit of Pleasure is Leaving Us Numb* (Nashville: Thomas Nelson, 2007).

Chapter 6: The Unquenchable Thirst

xii Prager, 31-36.

Bobby Schuller is an American Christian minister and writer. Most recently, he serves as the pastor for the Hour of Power, a weekly televised church service to millions around the world. He also serves as the teaching pastor of the Tree of Life Community in Orange, CA, and as the president of the St Patrick Project, a social services outreach in Orange County, CA. He has been featured on TV shows like Canada's *100 Huntley Street* and The Learning Channels, *The Messengers*. Notably, he was the youngest serving chaplain in the Chautauqua Institute's one hundred fifty year history.

Bobby graduated from Oral Roberts University in 2003 and received his Master of Divinity degree from Fuller Theological Seminary in 2008. He currently resides in Orange, CA with his wife Hannah and their two children, Haven and Cohen.